GLADSTONE AND DISRAELI
PRINCIPLES AND POLICIES

Michael Willis
Brentwood School, Essex

CAMBRIDGE
UNIVERSITY PRESS

PUBLISHED BY THE PRESS SYNDICATE OF THE UNIVERSITY OF CAMBRIDGE
The Pitt Building, Trumpington Street, Cambridge CB2 1RP, United Kingdom

CAMBRIDGE UNIVERSITY PRESS
The Edinburgh Building, Cambridge CB2 2RU, United Kingdom
40 West 20th Street, New York, NY 10011–4211, USA
10 Stamford Road, Oakleigh, Melbourne 3166, Australia

First published 1989
Reprinted 1997

Printed in the United Kingdom at the University Press, Cambridge

A catalogue record for this book is available from the British Library

Library of Congress Cataloguing in Publication data

Willis, Michael
    Gladstone and Disraeli: principles and policies / Michael Willis.
    (Cambridge topics in history)
    1. Disraeli, Benjamin, Earl of Beaconsfield, 1804–1881.
2. Gladstone, W. E. (William Ewart), 1809–1898.   3. Great Britain –
Politics and government – 1837–1901.   I. Title.   II. Series.
DA564.B3W55 1989
941.081´092´2 – dc19   88–25666
                                                             CIP

ISBN 0 521 36805 7 paperback

I am grateful to the series editors and Stephanie Boyd of CUP for
their advice, to Dr J. P. Parry for reading the Introduction, and
to Professor J. Vincent for some of the thoughts at the beginning
of the Introduction which came from his lecture 'Was Gladstone
a Failure?'

Cover illustration Details of portraits of William Ewart Gladstone and
Benjamin Disraeli by Sir John Everett Millais, by courtesy of the
National Portrait Gallery, London.

US

Contents

Gladstone and Disraeli – table of their careers

	Gladstone
1832	Elected Conservative MP
1835	Under-secretary for War and Colonies in Peel's first ministry
1841–43	Vice-president of Board of Trade in Peel's second ministry
1843–45	President of Board of Trade
1845–46	Secretary for War and Colonies until the fall of Peel's ministry
1846–59	Part of the 'Peelite' group in Parliament
1852–55	Chancellor of Exchequer in Aberdeen's ministry and briefly in Palmerston's first ministry
1859–66	Chancellor of Exchequer in Palmerston's second ministry and Russell's second ministry
1868–74	First ministry
1880–85	Second ministry
1886	Third ministry
1892–94	Fourth ministry

	Disraeli
1837	Elected Conservative MP
1846	Opposes Peel's repeal of the Corn Laws
1852	Chancellor of Exchequer in Derby's first ministry
1858–59	Chancellor of Exchequer in Derby's second ministry
1866–68	Chancellor of Exchequer in Derby's third ministry
1868	First ministry
1874–80	Second ministry

Introduction

Gladstone and Disraeli: myth and reality

Gladstone and Disraeli are often considered the greatest Victorian statesmen: yet as politicians in many ways they failed. We generally reckon that parliamentary politicians succeed when they hold power, win elections and initiate great legislation, but by these standards Gladstone and Disraeli were only patchily successful. Gladstone was probably at the height of his powers between the age of 33, when he first entered the Cabinet in 1843, and 58, when he became Prime Minister. In this time he was in office for under twelve years and out for over fourteen. 'I saw great things to do,' he wrote to a friend in 1857. 'I longed to do them. I am losing the best years of my life out of my natural service ...' Disraeli was nearly 70 when he first became Prime Minister with the power of a House of Commons' majority behind him, in 1874. Up to then he had been in office for a total of under five years and always in a minority government. 'Power! It has come to me too late,' he complained in 1878. 'There were days when, on waking, I felt I could move dynasties and governments; but that has passed away.'

The electoral record was not satisfactory either. In his first ministry (1868–74), Gladstone led a Liberal coalition of Peelites, Whigs and Radicals who had enjoyed a parliamentary majority since 1846 and who had lost power only when they failed to agree among themselves. Few could have expected them to lose to a Conservative majority at the next election, but under Gladstone's premiership they did exactly that in 1874. Furthermore, in the last years of Gladstone's leadership, from 1886, it seemed that the Liberals were losing their role as the natural party of government to the Conservative Party, under the leadership of Lord Salisbury.

On the other side, although Disraeli achieved a great electoral triumph in 1874, he had helped to produce a Conservative split in 1846 which had kept the Party in a parliamentary minority for 28 years, and he had led his followers to resounding defeat in 1868. It is not surprising that a number of prominent Conservatives considered his replacement in 1872.[1]

Their legislative record is suspect too. Gladstone was responsible for some monumental budgets as Chancellor of the Exchequer from 1852 to

1855, and from 1859 to 1866. As Prime Minister he spent a long time discussing and writing about aspects of government reforms and supported them vigorously in Parliament. But he was only closely involved in the overall drafting of Irish legislation, and possibly a few financial measures. Disraeli, meanwhile, came to power promising a respite from 'harassing legislation' [2.5] and seems to have left the initiative to his ministers [2.13]. Despite their suspect electoral and legislative records, Gladstone and Disraeli are considered great leaders with prodigious reputations. How can this be?

Disraeli died in 1881, Gladstone in 1898: before the 19th century was out Disraeli's career had been romanticised and Gladstone's sanctified. Gladstone's portrait was incorporated in a host of domestic items from tea caddies to wall tiles. Disraeli's supposed political principles were commemorated in the Primrose League (founded in 1883), named after his allegedly favourite flower and soon boasting over a million members.[2] Many people even wore primroses on the anniversary of his death each April as a mark of respect for his extraordinary career. In the early 20th century the two men's lives were recorded in massive official biographies: Gladstone was enshrined as a lover of liberty by the devoted Liberal minister and political theorist Morley; Disraeli was presented as a great leader risen from unlikely and almost humble beginnings by *The Times'* journalists Monypenny and Buckle.[3] How have their early reputations stood the test of time and the pens of sceptical historians?

Historians' changing views of Gladstone and Disraeli

Morley presented Gladstone as a man who had slowly freed himself from a Tory upbringing and progressed through his life to a fuller understanding of liberty. Gladstone himself suggested this line when speaking during the last years of his Liberal leadership: 'I am a lover of liberty ... For my own part, as I have been a learner all my life, a learner I must continue to be.' But at the same time he claimed 'a profound reverence for everything ancient, provided that reverence is deserved', and several historians have recently emphasised the continuity and conservatism in his thinking.[4] Gladstone described himself as an 'out and out inequalitarian': he believed the competitive exams for the civil service, introduced in his first ministry, would 'strengthen and multiply the ties between the higher classes and the possession of administrative power.' He only reluctantly agreed to the abolition of religious tests at Oxford and Cambridge in 1871, and the introduction of the secret ballot in 1872, and he was less interested in extending education to the masses than in the religious issues involved in the 1870 Education Act. H. C. G. Matthew, the editor of the Gladstone diaries, argues that he believed much of the British administrative and financial structure in the 1870s might remain permanent, viewing his first ministry 'not as the new dawn of thorough-going liberalism emancipated by democracy, but as the setting of the sun at the end of the day of the building of the mid-century edifice.'

Gladstone became more radical as he grew older, adopting Home Rule later in his career, and towards its close contemplating the reform of the House of Lords. But much of the time it seems he wanted to reform in order to preserve. By removing certain abuses he might safeguard the best type of aristocratic government and the Church of England; by allowing colonies more freedom and self-government, imperial links could be maintained; and by granting land reforms or, later, Home Rule in Ireland, the structure of landownership and the British connection might be accepted by the Irish.

In a well-known biography published in 1954, Sir Philip Magnus portrayed Gladstone as a naive and high-minded man, more truly interested in religion than politics and totally different from other politicians. More recent historians have suggested that he may not have been quite so different after all.[5]

Gladstone thought on many levels and was intensely concerned with self-justification. Although at one time he thought it his duty to enter the Church, he seemed quite ready to convince himself that he should go into politics. How far he was then guided by conscience rather than political calculation is hard to assess.

Take, for example, his crucial decision to enter Palmerston's Liberal government when he was out of office in 1859. Gladstone himself justified this by his agreement with Palmerston on supporting moves for Italian unification. Magnus believes he was 'wholly sincere' and 'in the simplicity of his heart he was much troubled.' Shannon and Feucht-wanger agree that Italy was an important factor in his decision but Feuchtwanger emphasises how entry was an escape from political isolation and Shannon stresses his wish to regain his 'old office' as Chancellor of the Exchequer. Matthew, noting the absence of any great passage of self-analysis in the diary, sees the move as 'the hard-headed response of an able politician with a programme for action' and thinks it 'hard to see Italy as more than a convenient issue on which to combine with the Whigs on their own ground of foreign policy.'[6]

Similar problems of interpretation occur throughout Gladstone's career. Some historians explain his role in debates over parliamentary reform from 1864 to 1867 as being largely due to a concern to convince new voters of his political radicalism and to gain the Liberal leadership.[7] His support for Irish Church disestablishment in 1868, and Home Rule in 1886, resulted from much agonised reflection on Irish affairs, but both brought some obvious short-term political advantages. After a full investigation of the 'Bulgarian agitation' of 1876, Shannon concluded that Gladstone's intervention then was 'a case of mere opportunism'.[8] New biographies and the publication of Gladstone's diaries bring further insights into his actions, but he remains nonetheless a great enigma.

Soon after his death, Disraeli's political followers created the myth of Disraeli, the 'Tory Democrat'. In his novels *Coningsby* and *Sybil*, written during the early part of his career, Disraeli had described the problems of the urban working class [2.11] and called for a new type of Toryism to help the poor and to bind society together. In mid-career he had supported many social reform measures and had given urban workers the vote in the Second Reform Act of 1867: when at last he gained real power in 1874 he was able to implement a series of social reforms to meet the physical needs of the urban poor, and thus Disraeli's career seemed to show a remarkable consistency in developing a new vision of Conservatism. In foreign affairs, meanwhile, he had realised the importance of Empire before other major politicians, and his speeches at Manchester and the Crystal Palace [6.1] in 1872, anticipated the imperialist enthusiasm of the closing years of the 19th century.

This attractive interpretation was rather effectively demolished in the 1960s in Lord Blake's biography of Disraeli and Paul Smith's *Disraelian Conservatism and Social Reform*.[9] As these historians show, Disraeli was never a democrat. 'We do not, however, live – and I trust it will never be the fate of this country to live – under a democracy' he said in debate over the Second Reform Act. Neither, it seems, was he a great social legislator [2.13]: Smith concluded that 'the great Conservative champion of social reform and the reconciliation of classes came into office in 1874 without a single concrete proposal in his head'. Disraeli's emphasis on Empire in 1872 can be interpreted as a ploy to attack Gladstone's government, which was facing difficulties in colonial relations, and his foreign policy has been presented as a kind of rehash of Palmerston's in inappropriate circumstances.[10] Disraeli thus emerges as a stylish political adventurer, weak on policy and strong on opportunism.

There has been some reaction against these uncharitable views.[11] Disraeli's government did after all achieve a lot of social reform. He may not have had detailed proposals about how to get sewers built or slums demolished, but was this his job? Isn't a prime minister's role to set the tone of the ministry, to get the emphasis right, and to manage the political presentation, rather than to attend to the practical details of reforms?

Maybe his reforms were intended mainly as a gesture to the working class to show that the government cared about them.[12] Disraeli came to power offering a respite from Gladstone's controversial legislation [2.5], and reforms to improve the condition of the people presented a safer alternative to 'meddling' with the constitution or 'harassing' powerful interests. His social and political thinking does seem to show some consistency, but it may be better explained as the way in which a Jewish outsider could integrate himself into English Conservative politics rather than as a practical programme tailored to meet the needs of an industrial society.[13]

There is also some consistency in Disraeli's public speeches on Empire, though his private letters have been used to suggest that he did change his mind.[14] Were his well-known remarks on Empire at the Crystal Palace [6.1] an indication of a proposed future policy, or just a criticism of the Liberal government? There is further ambiguity about whether Disraeli was following a Palmerstonian policy. His handling of the Eastern Question may appear similar to Palmerston's [5.2, 5.13, 5.14], but his rejection of a 'turbulent and aggressive diplomacy' in a famous policy speech at Manchester in 1872 was a condemnation of the Palmerstonian line.

Comparison of Gladstone and Disraeli

Gladstone and Disraeli came to hate one another. This is partly explained by their contrasting personalities and moral standards. The middle-aged Gladstone reclaimed prostitutes whereas the young Disraeli had lived openly with a mistress.[15] On appointment as Prime Minister Disraeli rejoiced that he had 'climbed to the top of the greasy pole', whilst Gladstone thought that the Almighty seemed to 'sustain and spare' him for 'some purpose of His own'. Their hatred does not necessarily have to be explained by major differences of policy. How divergent were their political views and actions?

Throughout his ministerial career Gladstone tried to reduce taxation, cut government spending and restrict the defence expenditure which could otherwise upset the best-laid budget plans. Abolition of income tax was a long-standing ambition of his as both Chancellor of the Exchequer and Prime Minister. Disraeli lacked Gladstone's passion for finance and his belief in the moral importance of low taxes, but he too tried to keep down taxation and defence spending when he was Chancellor in the 1850s and 1860s. This was not, apparently, just because of his own departmental interest: as Prime Minister in 1874 he chose Gladstone's former secretary Northcote as Chancellor of the Exchequer, and appointed ministers at the War Office and Admiralty who were not likely to press for increased spending; the First Lord of the Admiralty, Ward Hunt, was a former Treasury Secretary, who had helped resist naval 'reconstruction' from 1866 to 1868.[16]

Their trade policy was similar as well. While Gladstone probably did more than any other 19th-century minister to achieve Free Trade, Disraeli helped bring down Peel over the repeal of the Corn Laws in 1846, and a few years later led the Protectionist Conservatives, who had wanted to maintain corn duties, in the Commons. But Disraeli, though the Protectionist leader, could not abandon Protection soon enough: the Conservatives dropped it after the 1852 Election and he never attempted to revive it.

As we have seen, Disraeli championed social improvement in opposition to the Liberals' emphasis on political improvement. But how different was his Conservative social legislation from that of the Liberals'? It is certainly possible to see some lines of continuity [**3.24, 3.26**]. In trade union legislation a clear difference appears. The Liberals' Criminal Law Amendment Act of 1871 prohibited peaceful picketing whilst the Conservatives' Conspiracy and Protection of Property Act of 1875 allowed it [**3.20, 3.21**]. Perhaps the change in thinking was not as substantial as this suggests, though, as Gladstone's Cabinet had considered reforming the law in late 1873 [**3.22**].

Gladstone and Disraeli were both prime ministers of Ireland as well as the British mainland: in 1871 nearly 5.5 million of the United Kingdom's 31.5 million inhabitants lived in Ireland, and with railways and steamships travel was not difficult. Yet although Gladstone apparently had a 'mission to pacify Ireland', he visited the island only once – for just under a month in 1877 on what was largely a holiday trip. Disraeli never went at all.

Disraeli's interest in Ireland was spasmodic, but he defended the Irish Church and landowners [**4.7**] and was concerned to maintain the British connection. Though substantially ignoring Ireland during his second ministry, he turned to denounce the idea of Home Rule as a menace 'scarcely less disastrous than pestilence and famine' in his 1880 election manifesto.

Gladstone was deeply troubled about Ireland in the 1840s and devoted much of his last years in the Liberal leadership to the cause of Home Rule. But his involvement was intermittent and demanded by circumstances rather than given by inclination. He first endeavoured to achieve Irish land reform from 1869 to 1870, by legalising a tradition – the Ulster custom, which gave tenant farmers rights in their holdings in only one part of the country – and declared himself strongly opposed to giving tenants generally 'a joint property in the soil'. Only reluctantly did he undertake a much more fundamental reform in the 1881 Land Act, and he proceeded to give Ireland more than four years of coercion. It is even arguable that he took up the cause of Home Rule in 1886 through force of political circumstance, and he would probably have preferred to leave it to others.

In foreign policy there was a clear divide – in theory at least. Disraeli's Conservative policy was to be 'national' as opposed to the Liberals' 'cosmopolitan' attitude. Disraeli's aim was to enhance Britain's power and greatness, and it followed that foreign crises would be handled according to British interests [5.2, 5.9, 5.13]. For Gladstone this was not adequate. He condemned the way in which action under Disraeli's government was 'to be determined by whatever we may choose to think to be British interests. That is to say, that our opinion of what we think best for ourselves is, after all, to be, in substance, our measure of right and wrong all over the world.'[17] Disraeli thought in terms of great power politics: Gladstone thought in terms of the values of Christian civilisation and sympathy with oppressed peoples. But he too was concerned with European stability and British interests. Although he condemned Turkish government atrocities vehemently, how much did his attitude to the Turkish Empire actually differ from Disraeli's [5.11, 5.14]?

Gladstone and Disraeli had strongly contrasting attitudes to the Empire [6.1, 6.2]. The concept of an oriental Empire fascinated Disraeli, whose mind was very exercised about routes to India [5.13] and who took great pride in purchasing Suez Canal shares in 1875, and acquiring Cyprus three years later. Gladstone thought this obsession with the route to India absurd [6.10] and bitterly attacked the acquisition of Cyprus. During his second ministry, Disraeli advertised achievements in safeguarding British imperial interests while Gladstone fulminated against the evils of the government's imperial policy, which he dubbed 'Beaconsfieldism' [6.9]. But this was a conflict in thought and presentation rather than substantive action.

The crises in Afghanistan, 1878–79, and Egypt in 1882, are taken as examples of how Disraeli's and Gladstone's ministries actually handled, or mishandled, problems of foreign policy (see Chapter 6). Disraeli praised the advantages of a 'scientific' frontier in Afghanistan [6.8] but how far had his government planned the manoeuvres which gained it [6.3–6.8]? Gladstone condemned the campaign in Afghanistan [6.9], but would he have prevented it? When the Russians encroached on the Afghan border region at Penjdeh in 1885, Gladstone gained an £11 million vote of credit from Parliament to cover military operations, though Britain and Russia then agreed that Penjdeh's future should be decided by arbitration.

The British occupation of Egypt in 1882 posed acute problems for Gladstone. It certainly was not what he wanted, but he led the government which carried it out and justified it to his Party and the public [6.11]. Some historians see the Egyptian take-over as playing a key role in starting off the European nations' scramble for Africa in the 1880s and

1890s.[18] The leading opponent of 'Beaconsfieldism' helping to precipitate the 'Scramble for Africa' would seem the final irony.

This section is not intended to argue that the clash between Gladstone and Disraeli was phoney or that their policies were really the same. It does argue, however, that we must not take their speeches and election manifestos at face value. We must also remember that the actions of a ministry are not just the product of its leader's policy but of a mass of accidental events, outside circumstances, and conflicting pressures. Gladstone and Disraeli were part of a broader political scene.

The Liberal and Conservative Parties

Neither leader could rely on the modern type of party discipline and organisation. At the start of his first ministry, Gladstone was aware of leading a parliamentary combination rather than a united party. Subsequent tensions brought the loose Liberal 'coalition' of disparate groups to breaking point both inside and outside Parliament [1.19–1.22, 3.9–3.12]. The Conservative Party was more united and better disciplined [1.3], but at the time of the Reform crisis of 1866–67 it was doubtful whether it would re-emerge as a genuine contender for national power, or remain a permanent minority faction as it had been for the previous twenty years.

Well-known national initiatives were taken to improve organisation on both sides, but their importance has sometimes been exaggerated. The National Union of Conservative Associations, formed in 1867, clearly had little influence in its early years: there is dispute over the importance of Gorst's appointment as the Conservatives' Principal Agent in 1870 and how far he improved on the party organisation which had gone before.[19] What is clear is that his organisation deteriorated after he left in 1874 [1.16] and that serious attempts were only made to improve efficiency in the 1880s. The Liberals' apparent reply to Gorst's national organisation was the National Liberal Federation, formed on an initiative from Birmingham in 1877, and spreading the influence of the notably efficient Birmingham Liberal Association which had been established in 1865 [1.17]. But here again its influence is questionable, and many borough Liberal parties seem to have developed on their own lines.[20]

While Conservative and Liberal organisations both aimed to increase electoral support, they differed significantly in other ways. The Conservatives' National Union and Central Office were formed on the initiative of party managers at the centre, and they were intended to mobilise national support for their leaders' policies. Liberal initiative came rather from the grass roots, from the Radicals and Nonconformists who had often developed local Liberal groups in the 1850s and 1860s, and who combined to pressurise Liberal governments in the 1870s and 1880s.[21] The National Liberal Federation developed from a National Education League which had fought to alter the education policy of Gladstone's first ministry, and it was designed to allow the Liberal rank and file to formulate policies and influence their leadership [1.17]. Politicians now found that they had to cultivate both their party activists and a wider electorate and that the two might not want the same things. The problem was greatest for the late 19th-century Liberals, and it is at least one problem they share with 20th-century politicians.

Evaluating the sources

We must approach any document with a series of questions in mind:

- How well informed was the writer?
- What do we know of the writer's character, personal background, opinions and political affiliations?
- To whom was the person writing or speaking? Are we dealing with a private diary, a letter to a single individual, a speech to Parliament or an outside audience, or an article for a newspaper readership?
- Why was the person writing? What specific end, influence or support did that person hope to gain?

These questions raise many problems. For example, writing or speech-making may be designed to influence a wider audience than appears. Politicians' speeches in and out of Parliament were reported at length in the newspapers, and a major politician could expect speeches to be printed in full even in hostile journals. At the Crystal Palace in 1872 Disraeli was addressing a wider audience than a Conservative banquet: in his Midlothian campaigns of 1879–80 Gladstone was speaking not simply to Scottish audiences in small towns and villages but to the British newspaper-reading public. Diaries and letters may not be intended only as private records or writings to a single person. At the height of his political career Gladstone had already seen the publication of many memoranda and letters written by contemporary politicians and friends.

Further, political affiliation was complicated. It may not be adequate just to label people as Liberal or Conservative. We see that the Liberals were a coalition of interests – there were great differences between Whigs and Radicals, for example, and between different types of Radicals.

There are more subtle problems too. Our whole mentality and outlook are so different from those of the Victorians. For example, it is hard for us to understand the religious and moral framework in which Gladstone thought and acted. He devoted much time to tortuous theological discussion, and his diaries show a kind of moral accounting exercise which can sometimes seem bizarre. Many Victorian Christians took up some form of charitable work; in middle-age Gladstone reclaimed prostitutes from the streets. When he became over-excited in a conversation, on his return home, he whipped himself and recorded the self-inflicted punishment in his diary with a little drawing of a whip. If this seems strange to us, it only helps to show how far removed we are from Gladstone's state of mind.

Another problem is that society in the age of Gladstone and Disraeli differed from ours in many of its assumptions, preoccupations and conventions in the use of language. Many of the sources are selected to show different value judgements which are not always easy to understand. For instance, opinions on licensing [**3.14 and 3.15**] illustrate extreme viewpoints, but their language is paralleled in other sources.

Political priorities were different too. Today, financial management and government economic and social policy are key political issues. In the mid 19th century Gladstone, as Chancellor of the Exchequer, raised finance as a subject of popular interest; but how far did economic and social issues form a staple diet of political debate and party conflict? The debatable similarity between Liberal and Conservative policies raises doubts.

Religious issues, on the other hand, played an important part which is hard for us to comprehend. Gladstone's religious preoccupations may have been an extreme example, but he could successfully unite the Liberals and fight the 1868 general election on the Irish Church issue, while at the same time Conservatives won seats in Lancashire on a sort of anti-Irish popular Protestantism.[22] The bitterness of debate on education and licensing [**3.5–3.16**], the motivation behind local Liberal organisations and the widespread debate on Anglican disestablishment [**4.1–4.3**] can only be explained by strength of religious feeling.[23] This was partly because of religion's moral and social consequences, but not wholly: religious truth and forms of worship were themselves of great importance – one of the most controversial laws enacted during Disraeli's second ministry was the Public Worship Regulation Act of 1874.

This book primarily looks at British politics. Economic, social, Irish and international issues are raised, but they are covered principally so that we can understand their impact on British politics. The sources are here for the reader to draw his or her own conclusions. But remember that the sources are one person's selection. These documents may suggest certain conclusions: another writer's choice could well suggest quite different interpretations. It is hard for historians to escape bias in their writing: it is just as impossible to avoid it in the selection of material.

References and bibliography

References

1   E. J. Feuchtwanger, *Disraeli, Democracy and the Tory Party*, OUP, 1968, ch. 1

2   M. Pugh, *The Making of Modern British Politics 1867–1939*, Blackwell, 1982 pp. 49–53 and M. Pugh, *The Tories and the People, 1880–1935*, Blackwell, 1985

3   J. Morley, *Life of W. E. Gladstone*, three vols., 1903; W. F. Monypenny and G. E. Buckle, *Life of Benjamin Disraeli*, six vols., 1910–24

4   E.g. D. M. Shreuder, 'The Making of Mr Gladstone's Posthumous Career: The Role of Morley and Knaplund as "Monumental Masons"', 1903–27' in B. L. Kinzer (ed.) *The Gladstonian Turn of Mind*, University of Toronto Press, 1985

5   P. Magnus, *Gladstone*, John Murray, 1954; J. Vincent, *The Formation of the British Liberal Party 1857–68*, Pelican, 1972, pp. 244–67; E. J. Feuchtwanger, *Gladstone*, Allen Lane, 1975; R. T. Shannon, *Gladstone*, vol. 1, 1809–65, Hamish Hamilton, 1982

6   Magnus, op. cit. pp. 139–40; Feuchtwanger, op. cit., p. 106; Shannon, op. cit., p. 383; H. C. G. Matthew *Gladstone 1809–1874*, OUP 1986 pp. 107–8

7   Vincent, op. cit., pp. 256–59; M. Cowling, *Disraeli, Gladstone and Revolution*, CUP, 1967, gives the classic 'High Politics' view of the 1866–67 Reform crisis

8   R. T. Shannon, *The Crisis of Imperialism*, Paladin, 1974, p. 129; and R. T. Shannon, *Gladstone and the Bulgarian Agitation 1876*, Nelson, 1963

9   R. Blake, *Disraeli*, Eyre and Spottiswoode, 1966; P. Smith, *Disraelian Conservatism and Social Reform*, Routledge and Kegan Paul, 1967

10 Blake, op.cit., chs XXV–XXVII; Shannon, *The Crisis of Imperialism* ch 6

11 E.g. J. T. Ward, 'Derby and Disraeli' in D. Southgate (ed.) *The Conservative Leadership 1832–1932*, Macmillan, 1974; and D. Southgate, 'From Disraeli to Law' in Lord Butler (ed.) *The Conservatives*, George Allen and Unwin, 1977

12 R. T. Shannon, *The Crisis of Imperialism*, pp. 104–5

13 P. Smith, 'Disraeli's Politics', *Transactions of the Royal Historical Society*, vol. 37, 1987

14 C. C. Eldridge, *Victorian Imperialism*, Hodder and Stoughton, 1978, pp. 101–5; and in more detail C. C. Eldridge, *England's Mission: The Imperial Idea in the Age of Gladstone and Disraeli 1868–1880*, Macmillan, 1973, pp. 178–79

15 Matthew, op.cit., pp. 90–95; Blake op. cit. p. 113

16 P. R. Ghosh, 'Disraelian Conservatism: a financial approach', *English Historical Review*, vol. XCIX, April 1984

17 P. Stansky, *Gladstone, A Progress in Politics*, Norton and Co, 1979, pp. 127–28
18 R. E. Robinson and J. A. Gallagher, *Africa and the Victorians: the official mind of Imperialism*, Macmillan, 1961
19 E. J. Feuchtwanger, *Disraeli, Democracy and the Tory Party*, ch. V; R. Stewart, *The Foundation of the Conservative Party, 1830–67*, Longman, 1978
20 Vincent, op. cit., p. 128; H. J. Hanham, *Elections and Party Management: Politics in the Time of Disraeli and Gladstone*, Harvester Press, 1978 (first published 1959) ch 7
21 Vincent op.cit.; also see D. A. Hamer, *Liberal Politics in the Age of Gladstone and Rosebery*, OUP, 1972; and D. A. Hamer, *The Politics of Electoral Pressure*, Hassocks, 1977
22 R. L. Greenall, 'Popular Conservatism in Salford 1868–86', *Northern History* vol. IX, 1974
23 On the importance of religion see J. P. Parry, 'Religion and the collapse of Gladstone's first government 1870–74', *Historical Journal* vol. 25, 1982; and J. P. Parry, *Democracy and Religion: Gladstone and Liberal Party 1867–75*, CUP, 1986

Bibliography

Although basic factual explanation and introduction are included within individual chapters, the documents and questions are best tackled after some initial textbook reading:

E. J. Feuchtwanger, *Democracy and Empire: Britain 1865–1914*, Edward Arnold, 1985 – good text book coverage of politics, and a useful bibliography
P. Adelman, *Gladstone, Disraeli and Later Victorian Politics*, Longman, 1970
B. H. Abbott, *Gladstone and Disraeli*, Collins, 1972
R. Blake, *Disraeli*, Eyre and Spottiswoode, 1966 – a very good biography
H. C. G. Matthew, *Gladstone 1809–1874*, OUP, 1986 – another valuable biography. It consists of introductions the author has written as editor of Gladstone's diaries and contains much complex analysis.

In addition to the above, the following books and articles contain valuable summary and scholarly research on the subjects of various chapters. A number of the questions given in this volume can be answered by reference to these works.

Chapter 1: The political scene
D. G. Wright, *Democracy and Reform 1815–1885*, Longman, 1970
J. K. Walton, *The Second Reform Act*, Methuen Lancaster Pamphlet, 1987
R. Blake, *The Conservative Party from Peel to Thatcher*, Fontana, 1985
F. B. Smith, *The Making of the Second Reform Bill*, CUP, 1966

A. Jones, *The Politics of Reform 1884*, CUP, 1972

T. A. Jenkins, *Gladstone, Whiggery and the Liberal Party 1874–1886*, OUP, 1988

R. Woodall, 'The Ballot Act of 1872', *History Today*, July 1974

P. Adelman, 'The Peers versus The People: the Reform Crisis of 1884–85', *History Today*, February 1985

A. B. Cooke and J. Vincent, *The Governing Passion*, Harvester, 1974

Chapter 2: Contrasting careers

P. Butler, *Gladstone, Church, State and Tractarianism*, OUP, 1982

J. Vincent, 'Was Disraeli a Failure?', *History Today*, October 1981

Chapter 3: Domestic reform

A. Bruce, *The Purchase System in the British Army, 1660–1871*, Royal Historical Society, 1980

E. E. Rich, *The Education Act 1870: A Study of Public Opinion*, Longman, 1970

B. H. Harrison, *Drink and the Victorians*, Faber and Faber, 1971

H. Pelling, *A History of British Trade Unionism*, Pelican, 1976

A. E. Musson, *British Trade Unions, 1800–1875*, Macmillan, 1972

Chapter 4: Ireland

G. Morton, *Home Rule and the Irish Question*, Longman, 1980

M. J. Winstanley, *Ireland and the Land Question 1800–1922*, Methuen Lancaster Pamphlet, 1984

J. C. Beckett, *The Making of Modern Ireland 1603 1923*, Faber and Faber, 1966

F. S. L. Lyons, *Ireland Since the Famine*, Fontana, 1973

Chapters 5 and **6:** The Eastern Question and the Empire

K. Bourne, *The Foreign Policy of Victorian England, 1830–1902*, OUP, 1970

G. D. Clayton, *Britain and the Eastern Question*, University of London Press, 1971

R. Millman, *Britain and the Eastern Question, 1875–78*, OUP, 1979

J. M. Brereton, 'The Penjdeh Crisis, 1885; Russians and British in Central Asia', *History Today*, January 1979

M. Cowling, 'Lytton, the Cabinet and the Russians August to November 1878', *English Historical Review*, vol. LXXVI, 1961

D. Judd, 'Gordon of Khartoum: The Making of an Imperial Martyr', *History Today*, January 1985

C. Danziger, 'The First Suez Crisis', *History Today*, September 1982

1 The political scene

The Reform Acts of 1867 and 1884

The political scene in the age of Gladstone and Disraeli was substantially set by the Second Reform Act of 1867. The Act itself was the outcome of a complex political battle. Following careful accumulation of figures and calculations, Gladstone introduced a bill in 1866 to extend the vote to householders paying £7 a year rent in parliamentary boroughs, and to other very limited categories of men. His bill was defeated on a vital amendment by a combination of Conservatives and moderate Liberals. Derby and Disraeli then took office at the head of a Conservative government, and Disraeli eventually introduced a reform bill extending the vote more widely to all male householders who personally paid rates in boroughs. His bill was subsequently transformed when he accepted a sequence of radical amendments, including one from Hodgkinson which added over 400,000 new electors: it ensured that all householders would now become personal ratepayers and hence meet Disraeli's borough voting qualification.

Undoubtedly the Act was a sweeping measure which nearly doubled the British electorate, but there is controversy over why such an apparently radical reform was passed. How far were the politicians guided by principle, how far by tactical advantage? Did they undertake major reform because of popular pressure from outside Parliament, or to gain parliamentary and party advantage? Some historians have suggested that pressure from reform meetings and demonstrations forced Parliament to accept drastic change. Alternatively the 'High Politics' school of historians argue that the making of the Second Reform Act should be explained by the inter-relationships and manoeuvres among a small number of politicians operating in Parliament, bearing in mind the influence of political principles and outside events.

1.1 Gladstone's explanation in Parliament of why he chose the £7 householder qualification

> £10 clear annual value, when you make the proper addition for rates and furniture, must imply that the man is at a charge for his

residence of not less than £16. I am safe ... when I say that the
working man does not spend more than one-sixth of his income on
his house. Therefore, in order that he may have a £10 house, his   5
income must be £96, or, in other words ... he must receive, at least,
£1.17s per week ... Many an able, industrious, and skilful workman,
using his best exertions all his lifetime, would and must fail to attain
to such an income. Accordingly, I do not think that a £10 franchise
can be said to be liberally and fairly within the reach of the working   10
man. A £7 franchise would work in a different manner. Adding 60
per cent, as in the other case, for rates and furniture, to the sum of
£7, it would come in the gross to £11.4s, which would represent an
income of £67.4s, or instead of 37s per week a little under 26s a week.
Now, 26s a week is an income which is undoubtedly unattainable by   15
the peasantry or mere hand labourer, except under very favourable
circumstances, but it is also an income very generally attainable by
the artisans and skilled labourers of our towns, though perhaps not so
easily in the country.

Hansard, 12 March 1866, vol. 182, 54–5

1.2 Disraeli's explanation in a private letter of why he accepted Hodgkinson's amendment

On Thursday night, Dalgleish gave notice of a motion for Committee
on Compound Householders, which, if carried, would have 'hung up'
the Bill, and which, as it was to be supported by all the Independent
Liberals and many of our own men, would certainly have been
carried. I prevailed on him, yesterday morning, to give this intention   5
up, but he informed us at the same time that he, and all his friends,
and many of ours, as we knew, must support Hodgkinson's
amendment ...
   I waited until the question was put, when, having revolved everything in my mind, I felt that the critical moment had arrived, and   10
when, without in the slightest degree receding from our principle and
position of a rating and residential franchise, we might take a step
which would destroy the present agitation and extinguish Gladstone
and Co. I therefore accepted the spirit of *H's* amendment ...

Private letter from Disraeli to the Conservative MP, Gathorne
Hardy, 18 May 1867, printed in G. E. Buckle, *The Life of Benjamin
Disraeli, Earl of Beaconsfield,* vol. IV, 1916, p. 540

1.3   The Conservative, Lord Cranborne (later Lord Salisbury), condemns the Reform Act

If the upper and middle classes had made up their minds to this
tender trust in the people with which they have become suddenly
inspired, seven years ago, or even one year ago, no harm would have
been done beyond that which might result from the particular
measure they were passing. It would have been a concession – possi-   5
bly a foolish one; but it would have displayed no weakness, and
would not necessarily have provoked further attacks. But they have
just fought long enough to betray the weakness of the garrison and
the poverty of the defences. The dullest of their antagonists perfectly
understands that they have not yielded to argument or to sentiment;   10
that the apostles of Reform who have the real credit of their conver-
sion are the mobs who beat down the palings of Hyde Park, or went
out marching with bands and banners in the towns of the North ...
    It is an opinion generally entertained that the nation is on the
whole 'Conservative'; not in the party sense of the word, for that   15
meaning has disappeared, but in the sense of a general preference of
our institutions to those of any other nation. We believe this general
impression to be true: but it is a most misleading truth. It does not
follow because the mass of the nation is Conservative, that therefore
our institutions are secure ... The feeble preference of even a large   20
and powerful majority are no protection against the hearty and
vigorous hatred of a few ...
    For the last twenty years, again, politics have been less attractive to
men of independent minds than they used to be ... The Conservative
party became famous for its organisation and prompt discipline ... led   25
by a chief whose Conservative connections were an accident of his
career, when they arrived at the year 1867, having just tasted the first
fruits of office after a long and dreary fast, they were not in a
condition to resist any severe temptation ...

Article published anonymously in *The Quarterly Review*, October
1867

1.4   Disraeli speaking on Parliamentary Reform, 1872

One of the most distinguishing features of the great change effected
in 1832 was that those who brought it about at once abolished all the

franchises of the working classes. They were franchises as ancient as those of the Baronage of England; and, while they abolished them, they proposed no substitute. The discontent upon the subject of the   5
representation which has from that time more or less pervaded our society dates from that period, and that discontent, all will admit, has now ceased. It was terminated by the Act of Parliamentary Reform of 1867–8. That Act was founded on a confidence that the great body of the people of this country were 'Conservative.' When I say 'Con-   10
servative', I use the word in its purest and loftiest sense. I mean that the people of England, and especially the working classes of England, are proud of belonging to a great country, and wish to maintain its greatness ...

Speech by Disraeli at the Crystal Palace, 24 June 1872, printed in T. E. Kebbel (ed.), *Selected Speeches of the Earl of Beaconsfield,* **1882 vol. II, pp. 527–8**

Questions

1   (i) What division within the working class does Gladstone argue that a £7 householder qualification would achieve [1.1]?
 (ii) Why would he want to make such a division?
2   How can Disraeli's letter [1.2] and Salisbury's article [1.3] be used to support:
 (i) the argument for popular pressure producing reform
 (ii) the 'High Politics' school's view that it resulted from the tactics of politicians seeking power?
3   What problems are there in using Salisbury's opinions [1.3] as evidence?
4   How far do the reasons Disraeli suggests for accepting major reform in 1.4 differ from those in 1.2? How would you account for any differences?
5   How does Disraeli's attitude to extending the electorate in 1.4 compare with Gladstone's in 1.1?

The Third Reform Act of 1884 extended the vote to householders in the counties on the same terms as the boroughs, but it caused far less controversy. What was its significance and why was it less controversial?

1.5   Gladstone introduces the Reform Bill in the Commons, 1884

Is there any doubt that the peasantry of the country are capable
citizens, qualified for enfranchisement, qualified to make good use of
their power as voters? This is a question which has been solved for us
by the First and Second Reform Bills; because many of the places
which under the name of towns are now represented in this House   5
are really rural communities, based upon a peasant constituency. For
my part, I should be quite ready to fight the battle of the peasant
upon general and argumentative grounds. I believe the peasant generally to be, not in the highest sense, but in a very real sense, a skilled
labourer. He is not a man tied down to one mechanical exercise of his   10
physical powers. He is a man who must do many things, and many
things which require in him the exercise of active intelligence ...

Hansard, **28 February 1884, vol. 285, 109**

1.6   Salisbury accepts Reform in the Lords

We, too, have ... admiration for the working men ... we, too, believe
that with a due and proper consideration for that redistribution, that
allotment of power which alone can furnish a fair and true representation of the people, they may, with perfect safety to the great
interests of this country, be entrusted with the franchise if they desire   5
to have it ... But the issue turns on a totally different question. The
question is – How is political power to be so distributed that all
classes may receive their due position in the State, that all interests
may be respected, that a true mirror of the actual numerical condition
of opinions in this country may be produced within the walls of the   10
other House of Parliament ...

Hansard, **8 July 1884, vol. 290, 456**

1.7   Joseph Chamberlain on the significance of Reform

Next year two millions of men will enter for the first time into the
full enjoyment of their political rights. These men are for the most
part your fellow-workers in factory and in field, and for the first time
the toilers and spinners will have a majority of votes, and the control,
if they desire it, of the Government of the country. To-day parlia-   5
ment is elected by three millions of electors, of whom, perhaps, one

third are of the working classes. Next year a new House will come to
Westminster elected by five millions of men, of whom three fifths
belong to the labouring population. It is a revolution which has been
peacefully and silently accomplished. The centre of power has been   10
shifted, and the old order is giving place to the new ...

Speech at Birmingham, 5 January 1885, printed in C. W. Boyd (ed.),
Mr Chamberlain's Speeches, **vol. I, 1914, p. 131**

Questions

1   Why does Gladstone argue that rural householders should gain the
     vote [1.5]?
2   What might Salisbury have meant by, 'they may, with perfect safety
     to the great interests of this country, be entrusted with the franchise
     ...' [1.6, lines 4–5]?
3   (i) How far is Salisbury's view in 1.6 consistent with his arguments
     in 1.3?
     (ii) Why might he think it safer to enfranchise working men in 1884
     than he had in 1867?
4   What does Chamberlain suggest is the most important result of the
     Reform Act [1.7]?
5   From your further reading:
     (i) What changes did Salisbury insist upon during the Reform
     discussions of 1884–85 to ensure that the House of Commons
     contained 'a true mirror of the actual numerical condition of
     opinions' in the country?
     (ii) Why were these important?

Electoral practices and corruption

The new electorate under the Second Reform Act voted publicly at the
1868 General Election, though the 1872 Ballot Act soon introduced
secret voting. Violence and corruption, which were traditional at elections, still continued to an extent. The worst corruption apparently
occurred in smaller boroughs – Bridgwater in Somerset, and Macclesfield, Cheshire, were exceptionally bad – while election violence was
probably most prevalent in small towns and country areas where there
was less policing. The 1883 Corrupt Practices Act, limiting election
expenses and paid election workers, had a major effect, but there is still
some evidence of violence, intimidation and corruption at the 1885
Election.

1.8   A Royal Commission reports on the extent of corruption at Bridgwater, Somerset, since the First Reform Act

It has never varied. Whether in the old times, when the areas of place and population were narrow ... or at the present time when all those conditions appear to have been extended to the uttermost ... It is always three fourths, at least, of the actual constituency who are said to be hopelessly addicted to the taking or seeking of bribes ... Rank   5 and station appear to make no difference. Neither do we find that the needy are more corrupt than the 'well to do', nor the latter less prone to corruption. It is the chronic disease of the place: – and not one political party is more or less than any other tainted with the malady.

Second Report of the Bridgwater Bribery Commission, p. vii, *Parliamentary Papers*, 1870 vol. XXX

1.9   A Conservative MP, Colonel Barttelot, argues for an amendment to the 1872 Ballot Bill

The real question upon this subject had never been fairly put before the constituencies – that was, whether they, as Englishmen, preferred the present system of open voting to the vote by Ballot, a secret system, now proposed. No doubt there were many hon. members who, influenced by political prejudice, were prepared to say that the   5 Ballot would be a great boon to many classes of the community; but not a man would come forward to say that he personally was afraid to record his vote unless he was protected by the Ballot ... Were the classes who had obtained the franchise under the recent Reform Bill less independent than the class immediately above them? This Bill   10 indirectly cast a great slur upon the working classes of the community by insinuating that they were unable to protect themselves in giving their votes; but he was prepared to contend that the working classes were as independent and able to protect themselves as any class of people in the country. The small shopkeepers were not nearly so able   15 to protect themselves; but the Government during the time that this class had power never introduced any Ballot Bill ...

Hansard, 15 February 1872, vol. 209, 475–6

1.10

Cartoon from *Punch*, 5 August 1871

1.11   The Chief Commissioner of the Metropolitan Police, 1877

Since the passing of the Ballot Act we have never had the slightest
trouble at any election that has taken place in London, and the places
that used to be the worst are now the best ... [in 1868] the Tower
Hamlets election was carried on in a general state of riot; we had to
have 400 or 500 police on the ground to keep the peace.   5

**Minutes of Evidence to Select Committee on Parliamentary and
Municipal Elections, p. 24, *Parliamentary Papers*, 1877, vol. XV**

1.12

A general election is fairly quiet now; but there was a time, and that
within living memories, when it was a thing to wake the sleeping and
recall the departed. A convulsion of nature could hardly make more
stir. Civil wars had kept more within bounds; and dynasties had
succeeded one another more quietly. All that was violent came sud-   5
denly to the front; all that was rank covered the surface; all that was
outrageous filled the air ...

***The Times*, 1 April 1880**

1.13   William Saunders describing riots at the 1880 Election

LEAMINGTON – At Leamington, the night before the polling for South
Warwickshire, thousands of roughs crowded the principal streets and
smashed the windows of several Conservative hotels, and the plate
glass fronts of shops, irrespective of party politics. The next night,
after the polling had been completed, crowds of rowdies again   5
assembled in the streets ... the Mayor read the Riot Act ... after
Chief-constable Lund had deposed upon oath that knives had been
drawn, pokers used, that his men had been struck down ...

William Saunders, *The New Parliament*, 1880, p. 231

1.14   From the Royal Commission investigating corruption at Macclesfield after the 1880 Election

In conclusion, your Commissioners have to state their opinion, that while corrupt practices extensively prevailed at every election into which they felt it their duty to inquire, and though, indeed, it seems doubtful whether a contested election has ever been fought in Macclesfield on really pure principles, the corruption at the late election   5
was far more widespread, and far more open than had been the case at any previous Parliamentary election, at all events, of recent years, though the bribes were, in most cases, trifling in amount ... of those who were proved before them to have received bribes ... a large number of them were persons who would not have accepted money   10
from the opposite side, but who thought that if money was going amongst their friends they were as much entitled to have some as anyone else, and therefore accepted their day's wages, or a few shillings wherewith to treat themselves before or after polling. This they took as a sort of compliment, and without any feeling of   15
degradation or idea that it would constitute bribery.

This attitude of mind in relation to money presents was, no doubt, the result partly at least, of the older methods of procedure described to us by some of the witnesses ...

Report of the Commission on Corrupt Practices in the Borough of Macclesfield, pp. 14–15, *Parliamentary Papers*, 1881, vol. XLIII

1.15   [see next page]

Essex Election Poster, 1885

WARNING
TO
FARMERS & LABOURERS.

It having been rumoured that certain TORY FARMERS have been intimidating their Labourers by threatening a REDUCTION of WAGES if the LIBERALS GET IN,

WARNING IS HEREBY GIVEN

to such persons that they have transgressed "The Corrupt Practices Act," and are liable to

IMPRISONMENT FOR TWELVE MONTHS

WITH HARD LABOUR,

and will certainly be prosecuted.

 Every Labourer is FREE TO VOTE as he PLEASES, and any one INTERFERING with his RIGHT of Voting, WILL BE PUNISHED with the UTMOST RIGOUR OF THE LAW.

HART AND SON, PRINTERS, SAFFRON WALDEN.

Questions

1 Describe and explain the cartoonist's opinion of the ballot in **1.10**.
2 What arguments do the cartoonist and Colonel Barttelot advance against the ballot in **1.9** and **1.10**?
3 Against what do other sources in this section suggest voters needed protection?
4 Referring to **1.9**:
  (i) Why might the working classes be 'unable to protect themselves in giving their votes' [**lines 12–13**]?
  (ii) Why might small shopkeepers be 'not nearly so able to protect themselves' [**lines 15–16**]?
5 Referring to **1.13**
  (i) What does the reference to Conservative hotels [**line 3**] indicate about election campaign practice?
  (ii) Explain the significance of the reading of the Riot Act [**line 6**].
6 Assess the usefulness of sources **1.11–1.14** as evidence of the effects of the Ballot Act.
7 (i) What does the election poster [**1.15**] suggest about employers' influence over employees after the Ballot Act?
  (ii) Do you think the alleged threat was a corrupt practice?
8 Using all the evidence in this section, what conclusions would you draw about the impact of the Ballot Act on the conduct of elections?

Liberal and Conservative Party organisation

Reform Acts posed new challenges for politicians. How could they develop a successful party organisation to deal with the enlarged electorate and what role should it have? John Gorst endeavoured to improve Conservative organisation as Principal Agent from 1870–74. On the Liberal side the Birmingham Liberal Association took a controversial initiative in forming the National Liberal Federation in 1877 with leadership from the Radical Joseph Chamberlain. The Birmingham Association, which was to be a model for others, was arranged with small electoral areas – wards – choosing a large central committee named according to its number of members – hence the reference to a 'Three Hundred' in source **1.18**. The National Liberal Federation and local associations on the Birmingham model were nicknamed 'the caucus' – a derogatory term for an American type of electoral organisation allegedly manipulated by small minorities.

1.16   Gorst on Conservative organisation

The principle on which we proceeded was to find out in each
Borough the natural political leaders, to evoke their zeal and active
co-operation, and to throw upon them the responsibility of selecting
their own candidates, and organising their own machinery. We helped
but never interfered. Our work was tested in 1874, and you will I   5
think admit that our system was not on the whole unsuccessful in its
results. My own official engagement with the Party ended with the
General Election ... I have had the misfortune to witness the whole
system, to establish which so much trouble was taken, gradually fall
into decay ...   10

**Letter from Gorst to Disraeli, 3 March 1877, printed in E. J. Feucht-
wanger,** *Disraeli, Democracy and the Tory Party,* **1968, p. 137**

1.17   Chamberlain on the National Liberal Federation

It will be not the least of the objects of the new Federation ... to
reflect accurately the opinions and wishes of the majority of Liberals
for the information of all who are responsible for party management.
By its constitution, membership is restricted to associations based on
popular representation, i.e., to those which secure the direct partici-   5
pation of all Liberals in their respective districts in their management
and general policy. The Birmingham Liberal Association is the type
to which all these organisations approach. The managing committees
are elected by *public meetings annually called in each ward, and open to
every Liberal resident.* Thus the constituency of the Association is the   10
whole body of Liberals in the borough ... Mr Gorst ... when addressing a meeting of the Metropolitan Alliance of the Conservative Associations, claimed that they had set the example which their opponents
were now following. It may be that the idea of the co-operation of
independent associations is common to both parties, but the basis of   15
the Liberal Federation is not borrowed from, and cannot be imitated
by, any Conservative organisation.
    Conservatism naturally works from above downwards, while Lib-
eralism best fulfils its mission when it works upwards from below.
The popular element is not the one in which the Tories are strong ...   20
the leaders are everything and the followers nothing ... Now, the
special merit and characteristic of the new machinery is the principle
which must henceforth govern the action of Liberals as a political

party – namely, the direct participation of all its members in the
direction of its policy and in the selection of those particular mea-   25
sures of reform to which priority shall be given ...

Joseph Chamberlain, *A New Political Organisation*, 1877, p. 41

1.18   A Conservative view of the 'Caucus'

Whilst we admit, from a mere electioneering agent's point of view,
the success of the Caucus at the recent election, we would never
counsel the adoption of that system by the Conservative party. An
ounce of experience is worth pounds of theory; and we need only
refer to the shameless bribery and corruption incident on all con-   5
tested elections in the United States where 'Caucus is King'. It is
sheer nonsense to suppose that an ordinary elector will take as much
interest in the choice of a 'Three Hundred' – to which body his
political conscience is to be hence-forth bound – as he will manifest in
the direct election of his parliamentary representative. If the Caucus   10
really becomes an integral part of our electoral system, its principal
effect will be to retard the education of the people. Aspiring local
magnates will seek election to the wire-pulling body, and Tom, Dick
and Harry will either vote blindly for the Caucus nominee, without
troubling themselves as to his views on the questions of the day; or   15
else, if they revolt from the idea of dictation, they may reject the very
best and most eligible of candidates simply *because* he is the nominee
of the Caucus ...

Anonymous article on 'Conservative Reorganisation' in *Blackwood's
Edinburgh Magazine*, June 1880, vol. 127, pp. 806–7

Questions

1   Compare Gorst's approach to getting popular support [1.16] with
Chamberlain's [1.17]. How far does Gorst's account suggest that
Conservative organisation 'works from above downwards' [1.17 **line
18**]?

2   Referring to 1.18:
   (i) What criticisms does the article make of the 'caucus' system?
   (ii) In what ways does the article suggest that it might threaten
   democratic values?
   (iii) What features of modern practice does it envisage?

3   From your further reading and source **1.14**, examine what type of interest electors 'manifest[ed] in the direct election' of their 'parliamentary representative' by 1880 [**1.18 lines 9–10**].

The Liberals appeared as a sort of coalition in the late 1860s and there were well-known disagreements between the Whig leader Hartington and the Radical Chamberlain in the 1880s. How far were the Liberals ever united into a coherent party?

1.19   Hartington's view on the Liberal leadership after Gladstone's decision to retire in 1875

> My suggestion ... was not exactly that we shd do without a leader; but that the Whigs or moderate Liberals shd have one, the Radicals another & the Irishmen a third. I think that there is hardly any important question on which the Whigs & Radicals will not vote against each other; Disestablishment, Household Suffrage in Counties, Education, Land Laws etc; & the position of a nominal leader seeing his flock all going their own way without attending to him, will not be comfortable. If each section had its own leader & its own organisation, it seems to me that there might be more real union & co-operation on points where we could agree than if we were nominally united; when each section would complain & quarrel every time the party organisation was not used to support its views ...
>
> **Private letter from Hartington to Granville, 21 January 1875, PRO 30/29 22A/2**

1.20   Joseph Chamberlain in 1885

> If you will go back to the early history of our social system, you will find that when our social arrangements first began to shape themselves, every man was born into the world with natural rights, with a right to a share in the great inheritance of the community, with a right to a part of the land of his birth. But all those rights have passed away ... Private ownership has taken the place of these communal rights, and this system has become so interwoven with our habits and usages, it has been so sanctioned by law and protected by custom, that it might be very difficult and perhaps impossible to reverse it. But then I ask, what ransom will property pay for the security which it enjoys! ... Property cannot pay its debt to labour by

taxing its means of subsistence. You must look for the cure in
legislation laying the heaviest burdens on the shoulders best able to
bear them – legislation which will, in some degree, at any rate, replace
the labourer on the soil and find employment for him without forcing   15
him into competition with the artisans of the towns – legislation
which will give a free education to every child in the land, and which
will thus enable every one, even the poorest, to make the best use of
the facilities with which he may be gifted ...

**Speech by Chamberlain at Birmingham, 5 January 1885, printed in
C. W. Boyd (ed.)** *Mr Chamberlain's Speeches* **vol. I, 1914, pp. 137 and
139.**

1.21   Hartington's private view

[Chamberlain] is going to devote himself chiefly to land questions,
and seems to be most keen about giving power to local bodies to
acquire land compulsorily, to be let or sold to labourers as allot-
ments ...
    He also says that he is going for graduated taxation ...   5
    He is also for free schools. In short, we are going as fast as we can
in the Socialist direction.

**Letter from Hartington to Granville, 5 August 1885, printed in
B. Holland,** *The Life of Spencer Compton, 8th Duke of Devonshire,* **vol.
II, 1911, p. 72**

1.22

I feel that my position in the party is becoming every day more
difficult ... the Radicals are so forcing on their opinions that there will
soon be no place in the party for less extreme men, who will have to
be either for or against the new doctrines.
    The only possibility of keeping the moderate men in the party   5
seems to lie in your taking a strong and decided line against the
Radicals. If you are unable to do this, my firm belief is that they will
go; and whether I go or not does not much matter, as I shall be left
alone.

**Private letter from Hartington to Gladstone, 8 November 1885,
printed in B. Holland,** *The Life of Spencer Compton, 8th Duke of
Devonshire,* **vol. II, 1911, p. 90.**

Questions

1   Why did Hartington argue that there should be no overall leader of
    the Liberal Party in 1875 [**1.19**]?
2   What does Chamberlain mean by taxing the 'means of subsistence'
    [**1.20, line 12**]?
3   What did Hartington mean by 'the Socialist direction' [**1.21 line 7**]?
4   (i) Which of the policies that Hartington mentions in **1.21** would lay
    'the heaviest burdens on the shoulders best able to bear them'
    [**1.20, lines 13–14**] and 'replace the labourer on the soil' [**1.20,
    lines 14–15**], as Chamberlain advocates?
    (ii) How far would these policies be considered Socialist today?
    Explain your answer.
5   Why would Chamberlain's views be objectionable to Hartington and
    the Whigs?
6   How relevant is the disagreement shown in sources **1.20–1.22** in
    explaining the Liberal split in 1886?

2 Gladstone and Disraeli – contrasting careers

Contrasting leadership

Gladstone and Disraeli both had to appeal to the growing electorate and respond to a changing political scene, but they could not respond in the same way.

Gladstone had already developed a mass following before the Second Reform Act and received his first great popular reception at Newcastle in 1862. Although his speeches outside Parliament were intermittent, they received much attention and could achieve great effect. He was probably at his most active and powerful as a popular speaker when condemning Disraeli's Second ministry in 1879 and 1880.

2.1 A member of the audience describes Gladstone speaking in St Marylebone, London, at the 1880 election

Surrendering myself to the prevalent sentiment, it seemed to me as if someone had touched the stops of a mysterious organ, that searched us through and through. Two more sentences, and we were fairly launched upon a sea of passion ... In that torrent of emotion, the petty politics of the hour figured as huge first principles, and the   5
opinions of the people became as the edicts of eternity ...

All through a speech of long tortuous sentences he endowed us with a faculty of apprehension we did not know we possessed. And then the peroration: 'You are shortly to pronounce your verdict, you and the people of these isles; and, whatever that verdict may be, as I   10
hope it will be the true one, I trust it will be clear.' We leaped to our feet and cheered; decidedly we should make it clear ... a frantic mass of humanity roared themselves hoarse for a full two minutes. When I stood in the free air outside once more, it seemed somewhat un-reasoning, all this ecstasy; clearly I had been Gladstonized; and I   15
voted for him at that election.

From article in 'Outlook' by W. L. Watson, printed in Lord Kilbracken, *Reminiscenses*, 1931, pp. 110–12.

2.2   Mr Gladstone addressing the electors of Greenwich on Blackheath

THE GENERAL ELECTION : MR. GLADSTONE ADDRESSING THE ELECTORS OF GREENWICH ON BLACKHEATH.

Illustrated London News, 7 February 1874

It is not difficult to see why Disraeli condemned Gladstone as 'a sophisticated rhetorician inebriated with the exuberance of his own verbosity' and referred to his 'drenching rhetoric'. Although Disraeli made famous speeches to meetings of members from the National Union of Conservative Associations in 1872, Gladstone's limited 'stumping' of the country appeared a novel tactic unsuitable for a Conservative leader. Disraeli could not use such methods.

Disraeli's contempt for Gladstone's oratory was parallelled by Gladstone's disgust at Disraeli's character. In 1849 he recorded how unsatisfactory it was to have to deal with a man like Disraeli, 'whose objects appear to be those of personal ambition and who is not thought to have any strong convictions of any kind upon public matters'. At the end of his life he told his biographer, Morley, that Disraeli was 'the grand corrupter' responsible for 'a distinct decline in the standard of public men' and a deterioration in parliamentary politics.

2.3 Disraeli's Cabinet minister, Richard Cross, gives a more sympathetic view

Disraeli's mind was either above or below (whichever way you like to put it) mere questions of detail. When the House was in Committee he was, comparatively speaking, nowhere.

In this matter his mind was totally different from that of Gladstone, who was a great master of detail; but on great questions of   5
principle, and on all questions of high and imperial policy he without doubt asserted his supremacy.

He was a perfect master of debate and of epigram, and his sarcasm could be as bitter as gall; all the same he was a generous foe and an open one ...   10

Viscount Cross, *A Political History,* **1903, p. 44**

Questions

1   What effects does Watson's account show that Gladstone's speeches could achieve [2.1]? How useful could these be to Gladstone politically?
2   Gladstone spoke both in halls and in the open air. What does illustration 2.2 show about the nature and size of his audience? Who are the men at the front of the drawing and what is their importance?
3   How useful is Cross' assessment of Disraeli [2.3]?
4   How far do sources 1.1, 1.2 and 1.4 support Cross' comparison of Gladstone and Disraeli?

Policies

How did Gladstone and Disraeli differ in the policies they presented to the electorate? Extracts from their election addresses in 1874 give some general indications.

2.4   Gladstone's election address

We desire to found the credit and influence of our foreign policy
upon a resolution to ask from foreign powers nothing but what in like
circumstances we should give ourselves, and as steadily to respect
their rights as we would tenaciously uphold our own ...
    I fear that the time has not yet come when you can anticipate a   5
diminution in the calls for legislative labour ...
    It is sometimes said, Gentlemen, that we of the Liberal Govern-
ment and Party have endangered the institutions and worried all the
interests of the country. As to the interests, I am aware of no one of
them that we have injured ...   10
    As to the institutions of the country ... I am confident that if now
the present Government be dismissed from the service of their
Gracious Mistress and of the country, the Liberal Party, which they
represent, may at least challenge contradiction when they say that
their term of 40 years leaves the Throne, the laws, and the institu-   15
tions of the country not weaker, but stronger, than it found them.

The Times, **24 January 1874**

2.5   Disraeli's Reply

Gentlemen, I have ever endeavoured, and, if returned to Parliament,
I shall, whether in or out of office, continue the endeavour, to
propose or support all measures calculated to improve the condition
of the people of this Kingdom. But I do not think this great end is
advanced by incessant and harassing legislation. The English people   5
are governed by their customs as much as by their laws, and there is
nothing they more dislike than unnecessary restraint and meddling
interference in their affairs. Generally speaking, I should say of the
Administration of the last five years that it would have been better
for us all if there had been a little more energy in our foreign policy 10
and a little less in our domestic legislation.
    ... There is reason to hope, from the Address of the Prime Minis-
ter ... that he is not, certainly at present, opposed to our national
institutions or to the maintenance of the integrity of the Empire. But,
unfortunately, among his adherents some assail the Monarchy, others   15
impugn the independence of the House of Lords, while there are

those who would relieve Parliament altogether from any share in the government of one portion of the United Kingdom ...

The Times, 26 January 1874

Questions

1   What are the main points of disagreement between the two addresses [**2.4 and 2.5**]? On what do they agree?
2   Who were Gladstone's adherents who 'assail the Monarchy' and 'impugn the independence of the House of Lords' [**2.5, lines 15–16**]?
3   To which area and to whom is Disraeli referring when he writes of 'those who would relieve Parliament altogether from any share in the government of one portion of the United Kingdom' [**2.5, lines 17–18**]?

Gladstone and his views on the Church

We cannot understand Gladstone without investigating his views on religion. Theology was a frequent concern for him and the relationship between Church and State was a crucial issue – indeed, at times, *the* crucial issue – in his political career. He summed up many of his early views on this in a book, *The State in its Relations with the Church*, published in 1838. Here he argued that the British state should give strong support to Anglicanism as the true type of religion. But in the 1840s this set of beliefs crumbled. The issues raised when Peel's Ministry increased the government grant to a training college for Irish Roman Catholic priests at Maynooth near Dublin, in 1845, were clearly important in changing his attitude. Gladstone resigned from the ministry over the issue and yet voted for the increased grant. Why did he change his views and how far did they change? These extracts from his writing and speeches go some way towards piecing together an answer.

2.6

In national societies of men generally the governing body should, in its capacity as such, profess and maintain a religion according to its conscience, both as being composed of individuals who have individual responsibilities to discharge and individual purposes to fulfil, and as being itself, collectively, the seat of a national personality, with   5 national responsibilities to discharge and national purposes to fulfil ... in respect of its extension, it should, for the benefit of the state, be the *greatest* possible, and we are therefore bound to show, in considering the above-mentioned national purposes, that the direct aid of

the state promotes that extension; so, in respect of its quality, it   10
should be the *purest* possible, that is to say, should be the Catholic
church of Christ ...

W. E. Gladstone, *The State in its Relations with the Church*, 1838, pp.
26–7

2.7   Gladstone on the increase in the Maynooth Grant, 1845

The occasion demands of us all, as a matter of social justice, the
surrender of something of our rival claims, and of our extreme
opinions ... if on the other hand is to be advanced the plea of
religion, shorn as it has been of a consistent and intelligible character,
and immoveable considerations of abstract duty are to be urged   5
against all concession, how is society to subsist in peace, and what is
to be the fate of our common country? It must be torn by hopeless
and interminable discord ...

Hansard, 11 April 1845, vol. 79, 551

2.8   Gladstone on the Burials Bill, 1863 (allowing Nonconformist services in Anglican graveyards)

If [a Dissenter] has access to the churchyard, or has access to it
subject exclusively and absolutely to the condition of having the
service of the Church read over his remains, I confess I do not think
that that is a state of the law which is consistent with those principles
of civil and religious freedom on which, for a series of years, our   5
legislation has been based ...

Hansard, 15 April 1863, vol. 170, 153

2.9   Gladstone on the Abolition of Church Rates, 1868 (removing a compulsory charge for maintenance of local parish churches)

I own my personal opinion is that for all practical purposes the
Church of England would be greatly – not weakened, but streng-
thened and confirmed, by removing wholly out of action and out of
view all petty causes of irritation and disaffection, such as those
which arise from time to time in the attempt to administer the law of   5
church rates ...

Hansard, 19 February 1868, vol. 190, 964

2.10

Scarcely had my work [*The State in its Relations with the Church*] issued from the press when I became aware that there was no party, no section of a party, no individual person probably in the House of Commons, who was prepared to act upon it. I found myself the last man on the sinking ship ...   5
        There was an error ... in my estimate of English Nonconformity. I remember the astonishment with which at some period, – I think in 1851–2, – after ascertaining the vast addition which had been made to the number of churches in the country, I discovered that the multi- plication of chapels, among those not belonging to the Church of   10 England, had been more rapid still ...

W. E. Gladstone, *A Chapter of Autobiography*, 1868, pp. 25 and 55

Questions

1   Referring to **2.6**:
    (i)   What does Gladstone mean when he refers to the governing body or state as 'being itself, collectively, the seat of a national personality, with national responsibilities to discharge and natio- nal purposes to fulfil' [**lines 5–6**]?
    (ii) How could the 'direct aid of the state' [**lines 9–10**] promote the extension of a national religion as Gladstone advocates?
    (iii) What does Gladstone mean by 'the Catholic church of Christ'- [**lines 11–12**]?
    (iv) What would be wrong with supporting non-Anglican churches according to the philosophy expressed in this extract?
2   What reasons does Gladstone give in sources **2.7–2.10** for changing his mind about the strong and exclusive support which he thought the state should give Anglican religion in *The State in its Relations with the Church*? How far were these changes based on abstract thinking and how far on practical considerations?
3   From your further reading and sources **2.6–2.10**:
        How consistent was Gladstone in his attitude to religion up to the time of his first ministry?
4   From your further reading find out which reforms reduced Anglican privileges during Gladstone's first ministry and how far Gladstone personally favoured these? (See **4.3** on one of these reforms.)

Disraeli and his views on the Poor

Disraeli expressed concern about conditions in the large towns and sympathy for the Poor in novels and speeches at different times in his career. How substantial was his commitment to the 'Condition of England' question?

2.11   In his novel *Sybil*, published in 1845, Disraeli describes how an abandoned child grew up in the factory town of Mowbray

At two years of age, his mother being lost sight of ... he was sent out in the street to 'play', in order to be run over ... Three months 'play' in the streets got rid of this tender company, shoeless, half-naked, and uncombed, whose age varied from two to five years ... The nameless one would not disappear ... They gave him no food; he   5
foraged for himself, and shared with the dogs the garbage of the streets. But still he lived; stunted and pale, he defied even the fatal fever which was the only habitant of his cellar that never quitted it. And slumbering at night on a bed of mouldering straw, his only protection against the plashy surface of his den, with a dung-heap at   10
his head, and a cesspool at his feet, he still clung to the only roof which shielded him from the tempest.

At length, when the nameless one had completed his fifth year, the pest which never quitted the nest of cellars of which he was a citizen, raged in the quarter with such intensity, that the extinction of its   15
swarming population was menaced. The haunt of this child was peculiarly visited. All the children gradually sickened except himself; and one night when he returned home he found the old woman herself dead, and surrounded only by corpses. The child before this had slept on the same bed of straw with a corpse, but then there were   20
also breathing beings for his companions. A night passed only with corpses seemed to him in itself a kind of death. He stole out of the cellar, quitted the quarter of pestilence, and after much wandering lay down near the door of a factory. Fortune had guided him ... A child was wanting in the Wadding Hole, a place for the manufacture of   25
waste and damaged cotton, the refuse of the mills, which is here worked up into counterpanes and coverlets. The nameless one was preferred to the vacant post, received even a salary, more than that, a name; for as he had none, he was christened on the spot DEVILSDUST.   30

B. Disraeli, *Sybil*, 1845

2.12   Disraeli outlines Conservative policy in a major speech at Manchester in 1872

In attempting to legislate upon social matters the great object is to be practical – to have before us some distinct aims and some distinct means by which they can be accomplished.

Gentlemen, I think public attention as regards these matters ought to be concentrated upon sanitary legislation. That is a wide subject,   5
and, if properly treated, comprises almost every consideration which has a just claim upon legislative interference. Pure air, pure water, the inspection of unhealthy habitations, the adulteration of food, these and many kindred matters may be legitimately dealt with by the Legislature ...   10

A great scholar and a great wit, 300 years ago, said that, in his opinion, there was a great mistake in the Vulgate, which as you all know is the Latin translation of the Holy Scriptures, and that, instead of saying 'Vanity of vanities, all is vanity' – *Vanitas vanitatum omnia vanitas* – the wise and witty King really said *Sanitas sanitatum, omnia*   15
sanitas. Gentlemen, it is impossible to overrate the importance of the subject. After all, the first consideration of a minister should be the health of the people. A land may be covered with historic trophies ... but gentlemen, if the population every ten years decreases, and the stature of the race every ten years diminishes, the history of that   20
country will soon be the history of the past.

B. Disraeli, 3 April 1872, printed in T. E. Kebbel (ed.), *Selected Speeches of the Earl of Beaconsfield* vol. II, 1882, pp. 511–12

2.13   The Home Secretary, Richard Cross, describes a Cabinet meeting just after Disraeli had gained power in 1874

When the Cabinet came to discuss the Queen's Speech, I was, I confess, disappointed at the want of originality shown by the Prime Minister. From all his speeches, I had quite expected that his mind was full of legislative schemes, but such did not prove to be the case; on the contrary, he had to entirely rely on the various suggestions of   5
his colleagues, and as they themselves had only just come into office, and that suddenly, there was some difficulty in framing the Queen's speech.

Viscount Cross, *A Political History*, 1903

2.14

A REAL CONSERVATIVE REVIVAL.

"WE HAVE LITTLE OR NO *FISH*, GENTLEMEN; BUT AT LEAST WE HAVE REVIVED THAT GREAT AND
CONSERVATIVE INSTITUTION, *THE MINISTERIAL FISH-DINNER!!!*"

Cartoon from *Punch*, 8 August 1874

Questions

1   What do sources **2.11** and **2.12** suggest about Disraeli's humanitarianism and his political motivation in approaching the condition of the working class?

2   What are the problems in using a novel such as *Sybil* [**2.11**] as an indicator of a politician's views on policy?

3   How far is the statement on Conservative policy in **2.12** an appropriate political response to the conditions described in **2.11**?

4   What comment is the cartoon [**2.14**] making on legislation at the start of Disraeli's second ministry?

5   At Manchester Disraeli spoke of the need to be practical – to have 'some distinct aims and some distinct means by which they can be accomplished.' [**2.12, lines** 2–3]. From the evidence given here, and from your own further reading, how far did he have these?

6   Assess the record of Disraeli's second ministry in social reform, 1874–76, with reference to the problems and objectives mentioned in sources **2.11** and **2.12**. (Sources **3.23–3.26** give some further relevant material.)

3 Domestic reform

Gladstone's first ministry (1868–74) was one of the greatest reforming administrations of the 19th century, but not one of the most popular. Conflicting values and interest groups often made any consensus about reform impossible. Why did the ministry undertake such great and controversial measures? What were the competing values and interest groups involved and how far did the Liberal approach differ from that of their Conservative opponents?

Military reform

In 1871, the Liberal government decided to abolish the purchase of officers' commissions in the army. This was as a consequence of other reforms to achieve military economies, rather than because of any predetermined plan. Although Disraeli accepted the reform in principle, it roused strong opposition in both Houses of Parliament, suffering defeat in the House of Lords and being implemented by royal warrant. The issue had been discussed and investigated for many years: what was the case for reform?

3.1 The Report of Commissioners inquiring into the system of Purchase and Sale of Commissions in the Army, 1857

> Under such regulations there is little inducement for officers to acquire proficiency in the science of war, or to study the military progress of other nations. An officer who performs his routine duties, and who keeps a sum of money available to purchase his promotion, as opportunities offer, may look forward with confidence to the 5
> attainment of high military rank. While the subaltern who has not the means to buy advancement may serve during all the best years of his life in distant stations and in deadly climates, yet he must be prepared to see his juniors pass over him, for he will find that knowledge of military science and attention to regimental duties do not avail 10
> him, unless he is able to buy the rank to which his qualifications entitle him.

> *Parliamentary Papers*, 1857 (Session 2), vol. XVIII, p. xxii

3.2

SHOPPING!

Cartoon from *Punch*, February 1855

3.3   Gladstone discussing the effects of the 1870 Franco–Prussian War in an anonymous article, *Germany, France and England* ●

There is one consequential change which we must take for granted – a disposition to approach to, or borrow from, the military system of Prussia ... It works by short service and large reserves. It interferes very little with domestic ties. The system it employs for the choice of officers secures the highest efficiency for that capital and governing   5 element of the service, by a severe and practical training, without being open to the objections that attach to mere promotion from the ranks. It can hardly be doubted that other countries, and that we ourselves, shall endeavour to learn all we can from the Prussian system ... Lastly, Parliament and the country will, without doubt,   10 remember that among the features of the German system none is more marked than its economy; and the same principle, with due allowance for the greater cost of labour, and of free labour, will, we trust, be steadily kept in view.

The Edinburgh Review, October 1870, vol. 132, pp. 584–85

3.4   Gladstone supporting reform in the Commons, 1871

What are the officers of the Army? They are the brains of the Army, without ceasing to form a most important portion of its manual force. Is it an easy matter; is it a matter to be done without thought; is it to come by accident, that you are to have officers in your Army raised to the highest degree of perfection? How has the Prussian army been   5 formed? It is not the work of to-day, it has taken half a century to make the Prussian army what it is ... I hold that without the very best system for our officers all other improvements must be looked upon as dust in the balance, because they will want the living centre on which to depend ...   10

If we have been raising the pay of the soldier, if we have been shortening his service, if we have been endeavouring to improve his condition, if we are so ambitious as even to seek to draw him from a far better and more desirable class than that in which the recruit has in former times been found, it is not that he may have inefficient and   15 ill-trained officers to command him. The idea is to have the very best men and the very best officers ...

Hansard, 17 March 1871, vol. 205, 256–57

Questions

1 How do sources 3.1 and 3.2 suggest that the purchase system led to a less efficient and professional army?
2 Why does Gladstone consider that the abolition of purchase is necessary for the success of other military reforms [3.4]?
3 What indications do sources 3.3 and 3.4 give of Gladstone's principles of leadership and administration?
4 With reference to your further reading, why did (i) the Crimean War and (ii) the Franco–Prussian War suggest a need for reform in the British officer corps?

Education

Up to 1870 elementary education was largely provided by societies and individuals who raised and gave money on a voluntary basis, mainly for religious reasons. The voluntary schools they set up were then partly supported by government grants, and most of them were Anglican. As it frequently happened that no other education was available, many Nonconformist parents sent their children to Anglican schools. When the school received money from government grants they could then make use of a conscience clause to withdraw them from Anglican religious lessons.

The 1870 Education Act, designed to extend schooling and deal with the inadequacies of the existing system, was one of the most controversial and maligned of the ministry. Why did educationalists and politicians argue for and against change and how different were their motives?

3.5   From a Report on Schools for the Poorer Classes in Liverpool, by a School Inspector, D. R. Fearon

The number of children of the poorer classes requiring schooling in Liverpool is, on the highest calculation, 90,000; on the lowest, 73,100. But the number of children of these classes on the roll of all sorts of schools is only 60,000; so that, on the highest calculation, there are 30,000, and on the lowest, 13,000 children of the poorer classes in Liverpool who are not on the roll of any school whatever. Looking to the tendency, especially in private schools, to overstate the 'number on the roll', it seems nearly certain that at least 20,000 more children   5

ought to be on the books of some schools in Liverpool than now are
there ...   10

**Return of Schools for the Poorer Classes of Children in
Birmingham, Leeds, Liverpool and Manchester, pp. 167–8,
Parliamentary Papers, 1870, vol. LIV**

3.6   A letter from the Revd G. A. Dennison, Archdeacon of Taunton, 1866

A clergyman of the Church of England has, first, to educate the
children of the Church in the principles of the Church of England,
basing all his teaching upon, and leavening it throughout with, these
principles.

This is his proper business in his school. If he sees his way into   5
admitting into that school the children of Dissenters, as very many
do, in order to bring them to be Church children, that is his second
business.

But it is not, and never can be, his business to have children in his
school whom he can either teach no religion, or such religion only as   10
is not the religion of the Church of England.

The Times, 12 November 1866, printed in E. E. Rich, *The Education
Act 1870, A Study of Public Opinion*, Longman, 1970, p. 32

3.7   Robert Lowe, speaking in a Commons Debate on the Second Reform Act, 1867

It appears to me that before we had intrusted the masses – the great
bulk of whom are uneducated – with the whole power of this country
we should have taught them a little more how to use it, and not
having done so, this rash and abrupt measure having been forced
upon them, the only thing we can do is as far as possible to remedy   5
the evil by the most universal measures of education that can be
devised. I believe it will be absolutely necessary that you should
prevail on our future masters to learn their letters ... From the
moment that you intrust the masses with power their education
becomes an absolute necessity, and our system of education ... must   10
give way to a national system ... You have placed the government in
the hands of the masses, and you must therefore give them education.

You must take education up the very first question, and you must press it on without delay for the peace of the country ...

Hansard, 15 July 1867, vol. 188, 1549

3.8   A Radical MP, Henry Fawcett, speaking on education in large towns, 1869

But compulsory attendance once facilitating the education of children now neglected crime and pauperism would infallibly be diminished ... for the country would never listen to the degrading doctrine that there was no connection between crime and ignorance. This argument would not fail to commend itself to the ratepayers, heavily burdened as they might be at this moment – 'Bear the educational rate for a short time; it will eventually lead to a diminution of crime and pauperism, and, with the reduction of these, the burden of local taxation will also be sensibly diminished ...' As to the advance of
· education generally, he would only remark that each year competition with foreign countries was becoming keener and closer, and English industry must succumb in the struggle if other nations had educated labour and we had not. Let the House reflect how ineffectual our vast material gains of late years had been to effect any marked improvement in the moral condition of the people ... he saw that during the last nine years the amount expended upon outdoor relief in the metropolis had increased by 130 per cent. Was not that a portentous fact? The more they spent in the relief of pauperism the more pauperism seemed to increase. Why not try to reverse our policy? Pauperism seemed now to feed upon the bounty of the State. Like unthrifty husbandmen, we permitted weeds to be sown and to grow up with the corn, instead of attempting to destroy the seeds of future evil. Compulsory education, if established, would only be required for a single generation. Let the nation once be really educated, and then they could do without a compulsory system ...

Hansard, 12 March 1869, vol. 194, 1221–22

Questions

1   The School Inspector, Fearon, thought children aged 5–13 required schooling. Why might others not accept his statistics in **3.5**, and argue against his conclusion that more children should be at school?

2   Whom is the Revd Dennison referring to in **3.6, lines 9–11**?
3   Using sources **3.6–3.8**:
    (i) Identify the social, political, economic, financial and religious
        arguments advanced for providing education.
    (ii) Which of the arguments would you expect to be most contro-
        versial and which most generally acceptable among the electorate
        in 1870? Give reasons for your answers.

The 1870 Education Act established local school boards which would
levy rates and use the money to provide a kind of state education where
there were gaps in the voluntary system. But the Act also continued
government grants to the religious societies which maintained schools,
and Clause 25 allowed school boards to pay the fees of children from poor
families at both school board and voluntary schools. Nonconformists
were furious at this continuation of state support to the mainly Anglican
voluntary schools, and at the way money from local rates might be used
to pay children's fees at these schools. What were the consequences for
the Liberal Party and what part did the Nonconformist revolt play in the
1874 election defeat?

3.9 Dr R. W. Dale, a famous Birmingham Congregationalist Minister, in a public lecture, 1871

For a Liberal Ministry ... to involve the nation still more deeply in
the policy of sustaining sectarian religious teachers out of rates and
taxes – this was contrary to all that we had a right to anticipate ... it is
a policy which relieves Nonconformists from their old allegiance to
the Liberal party and which requires us so to organise our political   5
power as to prevent the Liberal party from ever inflicting a similar
injury again on the principles of religious equality ...

I do not care to enter into nice calculations as to the precise extent
to which the leaders of the Liberal party are indebted to the Nonconformists of England and Wales for their present majority in the   10
House of Commons; but this at least is certain, that we are largely
responsible for bringing the present Government into power. We are
responsible for its continuance in power ...

R. W. Dale, *The Politics of Nonconformity*, **lecture delivered at
Manchester and published 1871, pp. 22 and 29**

3.10   John Morley, the Liberal MP and future biographer of Gladstone, in 1873

It is absurd to charge those who disapprove irreconcilably of the education policy of the government with breaking up the party. It was broken up by the government itself in 1870. The party, as the parliamentary votes of its representatives in the House of Commons attest, was hostile to the extension of the denominational system. 5
Liberalism in 1868 meant this hostility more than any one other thing. The assumption by the nation of duties which had hitherto been left to the clergy, came foremost among the hopes of those who had been most ardent in the cause of parliamentary reform. It was the first article in that programme of improvement and a higher 10
national life, for which, and for which only, parliamentary reform had ever been sought by sensible men. This was the centre of the party creed. The break-up which we shall see openly consummated in the course of the next few months, was practically effected by the men who came into office to resist denominational ascendancy, and then 15
passed a measure which gives to the schools of the Church of England about 73 per cent of the total sum provided by the state for the primary instruction of children.

J. Morley, *The Struggle for National Education*, 1873, pp. 15–16

3.11   Gladstone in a letter to a Liberal minister, 1873

I heartily congratulate you on your reelection. But the attitude of the Nonconformists means mischief in the future. I do not see what can be done at this moment but to avoid sharp issues. They have power to throw us into a minority, and they probably will use it: but they have not power to do more ... 5

Letter from Gladstone to Lord Frederick Cavendish, 29 August 1873, printed in H. C. G. Matthew (ed.) *Gladstone Diaries* vol. VIII, p. 379

3.12   Francis Adams, Secretary of the National Education League (a largely Nonconformist organisation opposed to the terms of the 1870 Act) wrote this description of the 1874 election result

Mr Baines lost his seat for Leeds on account of his views on the Education question. In some twenty other constituencies Liberal upholders of the 25th clause were beaten, owing mainly to the defection of the Nonconformists. It must be said, however, that generally the Dissenters had the greatest difficulty in breaking away   5 from their traditionary support of the Liberal party, and many obstinate adherents of the Government policy were sent back to Parliament from constituencies where the absence of the Dissenting vote could easily have turned the scale.

Francis Adams, *History of the Elementary School Contest in England*, 1882, p. 301

Questions

1   What do you understand by Morley's reference to 'the assumption by the nation of duties which had hitherto been left to the clergy' [**3.10**, **lines 7–8**]?
2   What consequences of the 1870 Act did Dale and Morley consider objectionable [**3.9 and 3.10**]? Why do you think they held these views?
3   (i) How well-founded was Dale's claim in **3.9** that Nonconformists were 'largely responsible for bringing the present Government into power' [**lines 11–12**] and 'for its continuance in power' [**line 13**]?
    (ii) To what extent does Gladstone [**3.11**] support Dale's belief?
4   How far does Adams suggest that a Nonconformist revolt over education was responsible for the Liberal government's defeat in 1874 [**3.12**]? How might you attempt to assess the truth of his claims?
5   Drawing on other sources of information, find out how important education was as an election issue in 1874 and what other issues influenced the election.

Viscount Sandon was the minister in charge of education in Disraeli's government. He criticised the new school board system in a Cabinet paper and was mainly responsible for a Conservative Education Act in 1876.

3.13   Sandon's memorandum on religious instruction, 27 January 1876

We have every prospect of seeing shortly between three and four millions of the Children of the Country trained by an army of some

20,000 skilled Teachers, aided by some 30,000 Pupil Teachers –
having received no special Religious and Moral teaching themselves,
uncontrolled like the regular Civil Service by the conditions of   5
Pensions, restless, over-educated, and dissatisfied with their position –
a serious danger to the State and to Society – and not unlikely to
communicate their feelings to their pupils – and all this the result of
State action, and contrary to the evident wishes of the country ...

PRO 30/6 72, p. 52, printed in P. Smith, *Disraelian Conservatism and
Social Reform,* **p. 251**

Questions

1   What are Sandon's objections to the school board system [3.13]?
2   From source **3.13** and your further reading, consider what type of
   education Conservative leaders preferred and how they could use
   state action to foster it?

Licensing reform

The conflict of values and interests was most acute over licensing reform.
On one side stood temperance organisations with networks of local
groups: on the other was the powerful Drink Trade interest, with
public houses throughout the land. A bill to reduce both numbers of pubs
and opening hours, introduced by the Liberal Home Secretary, Bruce, in
1871, was withdrawn amidst howls of controversy. A further compromise bill, which became law as the 1872 Licensing Act, was principally
designed to reduce drinking hours and improve policing arrangements.

   The Conservatives might also have introduced licensing legislation
had they been in office – a Tory Home Secretary spoke of 'more extensive
police arrangements' being necessary for public houses in 1868. The
1872 Act itself was not a matter for party dispute, though Conservative
leaders later mounted direct and indirect criticisms of the measure [2.5].
On the other hand the new law gained little support from the Temperance movement which considered all government proposals inadequate
and championed the Permissive Bill which would allow a majority of
two-thirds of the ratepayers to close all pubs and drink shops in a locality.

3.14   A newspaper for the Drink Trade condemns Bruce's Bill of 1871

BRUCE THE COMMUNIST

The Home Secretary's Bill as each day elapses is becoming better understood, not only by those who are vitally interested in it, but by the public at large. It is with no ordinary degree of gratification that we have seen the rapid organisation of the Trade in all its branches take place throughout the kingdom. Hitherto, believing in the   5
strength of their claims for just consideration at the hands of whatever Government may happen to be in power, the Licensed Victuallers, together with the Brewers and Distillers, have exhibited an apathy and indifference to the cry of wolf, wolf, which has been raised from time to time. From this false security they have at length   10
been roused, and all signs of lethargy and indifference have disappeared, and nothing but the greatest energy and activity prevails in every City, Town and Hamlet throughout the kingdom for the protection of their property and their rights as Englishmen, which have been assailed by the Home Secretary in such a manner as strikes at   15
the root of all vested interests, whether it be that of the Licensed Victualler or the landed proprietor who has inherited ancestral estates.

The Licensed Victuallers' Guardian, 22 April 1871

3.15   A Temperance newspaper condemns the 1872 Licensing Bill

The nation has been asking for protection from the evils of the liquor-traffic – from the sickness, poverty, and crime it brings into being – burdens heavy to be borne, and which tend to reduce the sources available for increasing the wealth of the nation; and the Government has offered ... a wretched abortion called a Licensing   5
Bill, evidently framed with a total disregard to the wishes and desires of the temperate, the virtuous, and the religious part of the community, and in accordance with the expressed wishes of those who live and thrive on the wages of sin, and whose whole existence is devoted to the demoralization of the people ...   10
    We regard sound legislation on the subject of the liquor traffic as of immensely greater importance than disestablishment, the repeal of the clause of the Education Act, or the Ballot Bill ...

The British Temperance Advocate, 1 May 1872

3.16 William Magee, Bishop of Peterborough, speaking on Licensing reform in the House of Lords

I entertain the strongest dislike to the Permissive Bill. I cannot,
perhaps, express it in a stronger form than by saying that if I must
take my choice – and such it seems to me is really the alternative
offered by the Permissive Bill – whether England should be free or
sober, I declare – strange as such a declaration may sound, coming   5
from one of my profession – that I should say it would be better that
England should be free than that England should be compulsorily
sober. I would distinctly prefer freedom to sobriety, because with
freedom we might in the end attain sobriety; but in the other alternative we should eventually lose both freedom and sobriety ...   10

Hansard, 2 May 1872, vol. 211, 86

Questions

1   Referring to 3.14:
    (i) What is meant in this context by 'the cry of wolf, wolf' [**line 9**]?
    (ii) To what rights and values does this source appeal?
    (iii) For what reason did Communism appear as a European danger in 1871?
2   Explain what is meant by, and comment on the phrase 'a wretched abortion' [**3.15, line 5**]?
3   Evaluate **3.14** and **3.15** as evidence of English society in the early 1870s.
4   To what extent do **3.15** and **3.16** argue from religious values and why do they reach different conclusions?
5   With reference to your further reading, how great a social problem was drunkenness in Britain at this time? How effective was the 1872 Act in dealing with it?

Trade unions

The beginning of Gladstone's first ministry was a time of crisis for the
trade unions. Trade union members' intimidation of non-unionists in the
outrages at Sheffield in 1866 received much publicity; and a legal
decision in the Hornby v Close case of 1867 meant that trade unions
could take no action in the courts against officials who stole their funds.
In these unfavourable circumstances a Royal Commission met from
1867 to 1869 to investigate the unions' proper role and legal position.

The key issues were economic. Should wages be decided by free bargaining between individual employers and workers in a free labour market, or did workers need to combine in unions in order to deal with their employers on equal terms? Were unions necessary to pressurise employers into giving a share of any improved profits by paying higher wages? Or did they make British industry less competitive by forcing up employers' costs? But the most controversial issues, politically, were the rights of the non-unionist worker and the question of picketing.

3.17   George Potter, President of the London Working Men's Association and a member of the Progressive Society of Carpenters and Joiners, answers questions to the Royal Commission

[Royal Commissioner] In the event of a strike, have you known any measures taken to watch men and prevent their taking work?
[George Potter] The means which we adopt is, of course, placing what we call pickets on the job where the men have struck ...
    The men who strike form a committee, and appoint some of their   5
fellow-men who have struck to stand by turns at the gate or doorway and just peaceably inform members of the trade that there is a dispute, and that it is advisable for them to abstain from applying for work, but if they go and apply for work of course there is no prevention.   10

First Report of the Royal Commission on Trade Unions 1867, p. 24, *Parliamentary Papers,* **1867, vol. XXXII**

3.18   From the evidence of Mr Alfred Mault, secretary of an employers' organisation, the General Builders' Association

Here is a notice received by a master painter at Nottingham from the lodge there of this union of house painters.
    'Nottingham United Friendly Society of Operative Painters, May   ⏺
19, 1866. Mr Barnsdall – Sir, This society knowing you have in your   ⏺
employ one man of the name of Carson, he not being a member of   5
the above society, and as this society will not acknowledge anyone who is not a member, we hope you will take such steps as will prevent an unnecessary collision between us and your shop as we do not wish to put you to any inconvenience whatever, if it can possibly be avoided. Your immediate reply will greatly oblige, respectfully   1(

yours, THE COMMITTEE. Address the Committee, Old Dog and Partridge, Lower Parliament Street'.

As this note was not signed by any person, Mr Barnsdall took no notice of it, and in a few days afterwards because he did not choose to discharge the man Carson, all the society men were withdrawn   15
from the shop, and he has to carry on his business with a few non-society men; and these non-society men, every time they appear in the street in the presence of the society men, are hooted at and otherwise annoyed ...

First Report of the Royal Commission on Trade Unions 1867, p. 113, *Parliamentary Papers,* **1867, vol. XXXII**

3.19   **Conclusion in the Majority Report of the Royal Commission, 1869**

We think that whilst conceding to such workmen as desire to exercise it an extended right to combine against their employers, especial care should be taken that an equal right be secured to those workmen who desire to keep aloof from the combination, to dispose of their labour with perfect freedom as they severally think fit ... it is the more   5
important that the law should protect the non-unionist workman in his right freely to dispose of his labour as he thinks best, because, standing alone, he is the less able to protect himself ...

PICKETING

It has been shown in evidence that these rights are most liable to be   10
interfered with by what is commonly known as the system of 'picketing'. Picketing consists in posting members of the union at all the approaches to the works struck against, for the purpose of observing and reporting the workmen going to or coming from the works, and of using such influence as may be in their power to prevent the   15
workmen from accepting work there.

It is alleged that instructions are given to the pickets to confine themselves to a mere representation of the case of the union promoting the strike, and to use argument and persuasion only, without resorting to violence, intimidation, or undue coercion. But although   20
such instructions may be given, it is hardly in human nature that the pickets, who are interested parties and are suffering the privations incident to the strike, should always keep within the fair limits of representation and persuasion, when dealing with men whom they see

about to undertake the work which they have refused, and who may   25
thus render the strike abortive. Accordingly, experience shows, and
the evidence before us leaves no doubt on our minds, that during the
existence of a strike, workmen desirous to accept work are often
subjected, through the agency of the pickets, to molestation, intimidation, and other modes of undue influence, and in effect are prevented   30
from obtaining employment.

Eleventh Report of the Royal Commission on Trade Unions, 1869,
***Parliamentary Papers, 1868–69,* vol. XXXI, pp. xx–xxii, printed in**
G. D. H. Cole and A. W. Filson, (eds.), *British Working Class Move-*
ments: Select Documents 1789–1875, 1951, pp. 567–68

Questions

1   Which different individual rights of employers, trade unionists and
non-unionist workers are in apparent conflict in these sources
[3.17–3.19]?
2   Compare the evidence and arguments on the operation of picketing in
these three sources.
3   What problems are there in evaluating the evidence in sources **3.17**
and **3.18**?
4   Assess the arguments on picketing and trade union operation in this
section, using any other available evidence from the 1860s.

Trade unions were given rights to take action in the law courts and
protect their funds under the 1871 Trade Union Act. The law on
picketing was defined in the 1871 Criminal Law Amendment Act and
then altered during Disraeli's ministry by the 1875 Conspiracy and
Protection of Property Act. Gladstone's Cabinet considered alteration in
1873.

3.20   From the Criminal Law Amendment Act, 1871

Every person who shall do any one or more of the following acts, that
is to say,
... 3 Molest or obstruct any person in manner defined by this section,
with a view to coerce such person, –
1 Being a master to dismiss or to cease to employ any workman, or   5
being a workman to quit any employment or to return work before it
is finished;

2 Being a master not to offer, or being a workman not to accept any
employment or work ...
Shall be liable to imprisonment, with or without hard labour, for a   10
term not exceeding three months.
A person shall for the purposes of this Act be deemed to molest or
obstruct another person in any of the following cases; that is to say,
... 3 If he watch or beset the house or other place where such person
resides or works, or carries on business, or happens to be, or the   15
approach to such house or place, or if with two or more persons he
follows such person in a disorderly manner in or through any street
or road.

**Act to Amend the Criminal Law relating to Violence, Threats and
Molestation, 1871**

3.21   From the Conspiracy and Protection of Property Act, 1875

An agreement or combination by two or more persons to do or
procure to be done any act in contemplation or furtherance of a trade
dispute between employers and workmen shall not be indictable as a
conspiracy if such act committed by one person would not be punish-
able as a crime ...   5
Every person who with a view to compel any other person to
abstain from doing or to do any act which such other person has a
legal right to do or to abstain from doing wrongfully and without
legal authority ...
4 watches or besets the house or other place where such other person   10
resides or works or carries on business or happens to be, or the
approach to such house or place ...
shall, on conviction thereof by a court of summary jurisdiction or on
indictment as hereinafter mentioned, be liable either to pay a penalty
not exceeding twenty pounds or to be imprisoned for a term not   15
exceeding three months with or without hard labour.
Attending at or near the house where a person resides or carries on
business or happens to be, or the approach to such house or place in
order merely to obtain or communicate information, shall not be
deemed a watching or besetting within the meaning of this section. . 20

**Conspiracy and Protection of Property Act 1875, printed in W. D.
Handcock (ed.)** *English Historical Documents, Vol. XII (2) 1874–1914,*
1977, pp. 659–60

3.22   From a memorandum the Home Secretary, Lowe, produced for a meeting of Gladstone's cabinet on 7 November 1873 (Gladstone later informed the Queen that Lowe had 'received authority to draw a Bill for further consideration').

THE CRIMINAL LAW AMENDMENT ACT

I cannot agree in the objections taken by the working classes to this Act. We are bound to protect them and their masters from the tyranny of the majority. But this Act is limited to the tyranny of working men and masters. They are made liable to three months' imprisonment for assaulting, threatening, or molesting master or men   5
in order to coerce them to do or forbear from doing certain acts with regard to trade. This is class legislation.

No one should be subject to these annoyances ... I would suggest that the law should be made general. It may be said that we should get no thanks for the change because we retain the same power. I do   10
not think so. The working classes are very reasonably jealous of legislation pointed only at them ...

I believe that this change, together with others, would be well received, especially if it were pointed out to them that the object is to place contracts for the sale and purchase of labour on the same   15
footing as other contracts.

British Museum Add MS 44621 f.130

Questions

1   (i) Which clause in the Criminal Law Amendment Act [**3.20**] would prevent any picketing?
      (ii) Why was this restriction considered necessary?
2   Which provision in the Conspiracy and Protection of Property Act allowed picketing and how far was it restricted [**3.21**]?
3   How does Lowe's memorandum [**3.22**] suggest a Liberal reform of the law would have differed from the Conservatives' Act? How satisfactory do you think Lowe's approach would have been to 'the working classes'?

Public health and housing

Both Liberal and Conservative legislators initiated public health and housing reforms. The recommendations of a Royal Commission on Sanitary Laws in 1871 led to the Liberals' 1872 Public Health Act. This

Act placed the entire country under Urban and Rural Sanitary Authorities, and a subsequent Conservative Act in 1875 then defined their powers more clearly. The 1868 Artisans Dwelling Act, introduced by the Liberal MP, Torrens, with Conservative government support, allowed local authorities to order the demolition of unhealthy houses, but amendments by the House of Lords removed compulsory purchase rights from the bill. Richard Cross, Disraeli's Home Secretary, was responsible for a second and more ambitious Artisans' Dwelling Act in 1875. This permitted local authorities to draw up plans for whole areas judged to be unhealthy in the large towns, and gave them compulsory purchase rights, while commercial builders were to undertake subsequent redevelopment.

3.23 The Royal Commission on Sanitary Laws describes health dangers in areas not improved under existing legislation

Stafford shows a confusion of old jurisdictions ... There is only surface drainage. Pigs are kept to consume the offal of slaughter-houses in the town, and cattle fairs are held in the streets. The water is contaminated by soakage. No control is exercised over the erection of houses, and fever arises from the poverty and abominable con- 5
struction of workmen's dwellings ... East Bridgford is a parish of 460 inhabitants, where fever is constantly recurring from bad drainage, and the guardians have utterly failed even to put the powers which they have in force. There is excellent natural drainage, and the place ought to be very healthy. The people drink the water of the Trent 10
after it has received the sewage of Nottingham. The wells are deep, but the soil is porous, and the drainage poured into holes called dry wells finds its way into them.

Second Report of the Adderley Commission on Sanitary Laws, *Parliamentary Papers*, 1871, vol. XXXV

3.24 Sclater-Booth, Disraeli's minister responsible for public health, introduces the Public Health bill in Parliament, 1875

MR SCLATER-BOOTH ... said ... the consolidation of the Sanitary Acts had been frequently suggested in both Houses of Parliament as an object desirable of accomplishment ...
The time had come for a consolidation of the law on general principles ... the Public Health Act of 1872 had been passed – an Act 5

which for the first time met the great difficulty of sanitary administration over the whole country by dividing the kingdom into urban and rural sanitary districts. It was felt at the time to be impossible to introduce into the bill provisions to consolidate the law ... The appointment of medical officers under the Act of 1872 had been   10 the subject of a great deal of controversy and dispute between the localities and the central authority, and it was hoped that this power might prove useful, and also conduce to economy in some cases ...

Hansard, 11 February 1875, vol. 222, 229–33

3.25 Richard Cross introduces the 1875 Artisans Dwelling Bill

I take it as a starting point that it is not the duty of the Government to provide any class of citizens with any of the necessaries of life, and among the necessaries of life we must include that which is one of the chief necessaries – good and habitable dwellings. That is not the duty of the State, because if it did so, it would inevitably tend to make   5 that class depend, not on themselves, but upon what was done for them elsewhere, and it would not be possible to teach a worse lesson than this – that 'If you do not take care of yourselves, the State will take care of you.' Nor is it wise to encourage large bodies to provide the working classes with habitations at greatly lower rents than the   10 market value paid elsewhere. Admitting these two principles of action, there is another point of view from which we may look, and another ground upon which we may proceed. No one will doubt the propriety and right of the state to interfere in matters relating to sanitary laws. Looking at this question as a matter of sanitary reform,   15 there is much to be done by the Legislature, not to enable the working classes to have houses provided for them, but to take them out of that miserable condition in which they now find themselves – namely, that, even if they want to have decent homes, they cannot get them ...   20

Hansard, 8 February 1875, vol. 222, 100

3.26

INJURED INNOCENTS.

Bung (*to* Bumble, *Vestryman and Owner of Unwholesome Dwellings*). "TALK OV 'ARASSING LEGISLATION! IT WAS OUR TURN LAST SESSION; NOW IT'S YOUR'N!"

Bumble. "A REGULAR CROSS, I CALL IT. MIGHT JUST AS WELL 'AVE THE T'OTHER LOT BACK AGIN!"

Cartoon from *Punch*, 6 March 1875

Questions

1   With reference to 3.23 explain why no one would 'doubt the propriety and right of the state to interfere in matters relating to sanitary
laws' [3.25, lines 13–15] by 1875.

2   What administrative arrangements introduced in the 1872 Public
Health Act did Sclater-Booth consider useful in 3.24?

3   Why did Cross argue that although the state should 'interfere' in
sanitation it should not provide 'good and habitable dwellings' [3.25,
line 4]?

4   With reference to source 2.5 and the terms of the Artisans Dwelling
Act, explain why Bung and Bumble [3.26] had reason to complain of
harassing legislation in 1875.

5   With reference to sources 3.24 and 3.25 and your further reading:
How far did Disraeli's second ministry depart from the principles of
laissez-faire, fashionable in the mid 19th century?

4 Ireland

In 1844 Disraeli defined the Irish Question as 'a starving population, an absentee aristocracy, and an alien Church, and in addition the weakest executive in the world'. Following the terrible famine of 1845–49, a reduction in population and some rationalisation in agriculture brought improved prosperity to the Irish people who remained. But more commercially-minded landlords aroused resentment by increasing rents, and agricultural rationalisation often mean unpopular evictions. Bitterness at the British government's inadequate response to the famine encouraged small-scale revolutionary movements. The Fenian Brotherhood, for example, formed in Ireland and America in 1858, was dedicated to overthrowing British power by violent means. Their violence both in Ireland and in England in 1867, alerted British politicians and public to Irish unrest.

The Irish Church

In 1868 Gladstone, who had long been troubled about the Anglican Church of Ireland, saw that 'materials' existed 'for forming a public opinion, and for directing it to a particular end' on the Irish Church issue. Certainly it was a cause around which diverse Liberal elements could rally. In April they defeated Disraeli's Conservative government on resolutions about the Irish Church in the House of Commons, and a general election was soon announced for mid-November when the Church's future would be the main issue.

In 1869, following his election victory, Gladstone proceeded to disestablish the Church of Ireland, confiscating its landed property and removing its right to collect tithes from the Irish people. Some Conservative politicians like Gathorne Hardy, and newspapers like *The Standard* argued that this had wider implications: for example, how secure were the established Anglican Churches in England and Wales, or even the established Presbyterian Church in Scotland?

4.1

PUNCH, OR THE LONDON CHARIVARI.—August 22, 1868.

THE RISING TIDE.

Mrs. Gamp. "O YOU BAD, WICKED BOY! I S'POSE YOU'LL BE FOR A WASHIN' AWAY *THAT* CHURCH NEXT!"

Cartoon from Punch, 22 August 1868. The sand castle represents the Irish Church.

4.2 Gathorne Hardy, Conservative MP

If principles are applied to legislation for other parts of the Empire they cannot fail to be applied here, nor are there wanting here those who have avowed they will apply them. Hon. Members for Wales are eager to apply them, plenty of hon. Members for Scotland long to apply them, and in England there are those who hate any privilege,   5
who are anxious to see those who are above them levelled in the dust, and who would pull down the Church of England with the greatest pleasure. I could quote Members of the House and newspapers in support of that assertion ...

Hansard, 23 March 1869, vol. 194, 2098–99

4.3 Gladstone claims that maintenance of the Irish Church Establishment only weakens Anglicanism

It is for the interest of us all that we should not keep this Establishment of religion in a prolonged agony. Nothing can come from that prolongation but an increase of pain, an increase of exasperation ... There may also come from that prolongation the very evil which the right hon. Gentleman opposite made it a charge against us that we   5
were labouring to produce, but which we think likely to be rather the probable consequence of his line of argument – namely, the drawing into this Irish controversy that English question which we conceive to be wholly different. We think so, because, although in the two countries there may be and there are Establishments of religions, we   10
never can admit that an Establishment which we think, in the main, good and efficient for its purposes, is to be regarded as being endangered by the course which we may adopt in reference to an Establishment which we look upon as being inefficient and bad.

Hansard, 23 March 1869, vol. 194, 2127

4.4 The English economist, Nassau Senior, visits Ireland in 1862

We enquired everywhere for the house of the Archbishop of Dublin, but no one knew it. At last, one man said, 'Is it Mr Whately you mane? Then I'll show you his house.'

It was near some of the houses at which we had enquired; but it seems the population of the Roebuck district is Roman Catholic, and   5 no one chose to admit the existence of a Protestant Archbishop of Dublin.

Nassau Senior, Journal of a Visit to Ireland in 1862 in *Journals, Conversations and Essays Relating to Ireland*, vol. II, 1868, p. 167

Questions

1   What does the Church on the cliff represent in cartoon **4.1**? Why should Mrs Gamp imagine Gladstone might want to wash it away?

2   From Gladstone's own statement [**4.3**] and what you know of his religious views from your other reading, how far do you consider Mrs Gamp's fears were justified? Give reasons for your conclusion.

3   How far was Gathorne Hardy's argument based on what Gladstone might do himself [**4.2**]? Who were those 'who would pull down the Church of England with the greatest pleasure' [**lines 7–8**]?

4   How does Senior's story [**4.4**] support Gladstone's view of the Irish Church Establishment?

5   Do you think that Gladstone or Gathorne Hardy presents the more convincing argument and why?

6   Evaluate the cartoon [**4.1**] as a reflection of British public opinion, and Senior's story [**4.4**] as a representation of Irish opinion on the Church issue.

7   With reference to your wider reading, how far was the Irish Church question of symbolic rather than practical importance?

The Land Question

Some recent historians think the role of the land question has been exaggerated in the development of Irish nationalism, and many analysts see overpopulation, rather than terms of tenure, as the root of the problem. Yet, from the organisation of a Tenant League in 1850, land reform was a vital issue in Irish politics, and in Autumn 1869 Gladstone turned to work on a new land bill.

4.5   Isaac Butt, an Irish Protestant lawyer who later started the Home Rule movement, describes the land problem

The position of the occupiers of the soil of Ireland is at present generally that of serfs, without any security either for their tenure or the fruits of their industry. They are dependent for their very means of existence on the will of their landlord, while the amount of that

which is called rent is regulated, not by any economic law, but by the 5
disposition of the landlord to extort, and their own ability to pay.

This state of things has originated remotely, perhaps not very
remotely, in the fact that English power confiscated the whole property of our island, and placed over the inhabitants alien and hostile
proprietors, without making any provision to secure or protect the 10
right of the old inhabitants to live upon the soil.

Isaac Butt, *Land Tenure in Ireland: A Plea for the Celtic Race*, 1866,
p. 6

**4.6   A private memorandum written by Gladstone, 17 September
1869, comparing Irish and English land tenure:**

Land Tenures in Ireland	*Land Tenures in England*
1 Tradition and marks of conquest, and of forfeiture still subsist	1 They do not subsist
2 Landlord does not find capital for improvement	2 Landlord finds capital for improvement
3 Landlord frequently absentee	3 Landlord rarely absentee
4 Landlords extensively object to leases	4 Landlords rarely object to leases
5 In the parts of Ireland not under Tenant-right, the law which gives tenants improvements to landlord is rigidly construed and applied	5 The law which gives the tenants improvements to landlord is mitigated, and even in some cases reversed, by local custom
6 Landlord commonly (in the said parts of Ireland) differs from tenant in religion and politics	6 Landlord commonly agrees with tenant in religion and politics

Printed in H. C. G. Matthew (ed.) *Gladstone Diaries* vol. VII, 1982,
pp. 130–31

4.7   Disraeli defends the Irish landowners in Parliament

They cannot be accused of rapacity who, it is proved, receive a lower
rent than the landlords of England; they cannot be accused of ruth-
lessness when the solitary instances with pain and difficulty brought
forward against them are instances of a very few men of crazy

imagination and conduct; and if we were to make a selection in   5
England in the same spirit, we might, perhaps, find a few individual
proprietors influenced by similar feelings ...

Hansard, 11 March 1870 vol. 199, 1807

Questions

1   What 'economic law' might Irish landowners cite to explain rent
    levels [**4.5, line 5**]?
2   What is meant by tenant right [**4.6**]?
3   Explain Butt's reference to English power confiscating 'the whole
    property of our island' [**4.5, lines 8–9**] and Gladstone's mention of
    'marks of conquest' [**4.6**].
4   What are Butt's main criticisms of Irish land tenure? What indica-
    tions of bias can you find in 4.5? How valid do you think Butt's
    criticisms are?
5   How far do the points in Gladstone's memorandum [**4.6**] support
    Butt's contentions?
6   (i) Why do you think Disraeli defended Irish landlords?
    (ii) How adequate is the defence in **4.7**?
    (iii) Why might Irish rents be lower than English?
7   From your reading:
    (i) To what extent did Irish tenant grievances arise from the actions
       of the individual landowners or the system of landholding?
    (ii) How far could the Land Question be solved by legislation?

Gladstone advocated Irish land reform at the 1868 Election, and he was
closely involved in drafting the Land Acts of 1870 and 1881, though he
only reluctantly accepted the need for another major land bill after his
return to office in 1880. What were his intentions? How far did his
legislation fulfil them and how far did it meet Irish demands?

4.8

The problem before us is, I do not say wholly but in great part, this,
how to make equitable provision for a security against the suffering
now consequent upon eviction, without subverting the foundations of
the relation between Landlord and tenant ...

**Letter from Gladstone to Earl Russell, 4 November 1869, printed in
H. C. G. Matthew (ed.)** *Gladstone Diaries* **vol. VII, 1982, p. 163**

4.9   Clauses from the 1870 Land Act

(1)   The usages prevalent in the province of Ulster ... are hereby declared to be legal, and shall ... be enforced in manner provided by this Act.

(3)   [A tenant elsewhere who] is disturbed in his holding by the act of the landlord shall be entitled to such compensation for the   5
loss which the court shall find to be sustained by him by reason of quitting his holding, to be paid by the landlord, as the court may think just ...

(9)   ... a person who is ejected for nonpayment of rent ... shall stand in the same position in all respects as if he were quitting his   10
holding voluntarily ... the Court may, if it think fit, treat such ejectment as a disturbance ... if, in case of any such tenancy of a holding held at an annual rent not exceeding fifteen pounds, the Court shall certify that the non payment of rent causing the eviction has arisen from the rent being an exorbitant rent ...   15

Note: The House of Lords substituted 'exorbitant' for 'excessive' in Clause 9 [line 15].

The Irish Landlord and Tenant Act, 1870

4.10   Gladstone reviews the 1870 Act in a secret Cabinet memorandum of 9 December 1880

Besides these changes, forced upon us by the controlling and obstructing power of the House of Lords, there was certainly at least one *lack* in the Bill, in that it placed no other restraint upon augmentations of rent than the compensation for disturbance ... Notwithstanding this weakness in the Bill ... it was received with unequivocal   5
satisfaction by the people of Ireland; it greatly promoted the prosperity of the country, and it laid the Land question in Ireland generally to sleep ...

Upon this (for Ireland) happy state of things, there supervened a series of bad seasons, 1877–79, the last of which, in parts of a few   10
counties, brought the people near to famine. While they were in this state there took place, most unhappily, a large increase in the number of evictions ...

Cabinet Papers CAB 37/4 81 WEG, printed in H. C. G. Matthew (ed.) *Gladstone Diaries* **vol. IX, 1986, p. 633**

4.11   Clauses from the 1881 Land Act

(1) The tenant ... may sell his tenancy for the best price that can be got for the same ...

(5) A tenant shall not ... be compelled to quit the holding of which he is tenant except in consequence of the breach of some one or more of the conditions following ...   5
1 The tenant shall pay his rent at the appointed time ...

(8) 1 The tenant ... may from time to time during the continuance of such tenancy apply to the court to fix the fair rent to be paid by such tenant to the landlord for the holding ...

Land Law (Ireland) Act, 1881, printed in W. D. Handcock (ed.)
English Historical Documents vol. XII (2) 1874–1914, 1977, pp. 304–5

Questions

1   How far do the clauses of the 1870 Act [**4.9**] give 'security against the suffering now consequent upon eviction' [**4.8, lines 2–3**]? How important was the Lords' amendment in Clause 9?

2   With reference to further reading:
How accurate is Gladstone's assessment of the 1870 Act's initial success and the reasons for its failure [**4.10**]?

3   Referring to **4.11**:
  (i) What were the '3Fs' conceded to Irish tenants in the 1881 Act and which of these was granted in each clause in **4.11**?
  (ii) To what extent do the clauses subvert 'the foundations of the relation between Landlord and tenant' [**4.8, lines 3–4**] which Gladstone was concerned to maintain in 1870? How far do they grant 'a joint property in the soil' which he opposed in Parliament in 1870?
  (iii) How far do the terms meet Butt's objections to the system of Irish land tenure in **4.5**? Why did many Irish people regard them as inadequate?

4   From your further reading, how important do you consider the land issue was in Irish politics?

The Land War, 1879–82

Between 1877 and 1879 falling prices for some farm products combined with crop failures to bring agricultural depression in Ireland. Tenants fell into arrears with their rents and evictions increased. In these circumstances, a group known as the Fenians, who advocated violent revolution, joined with Irish MPs, who had been using parliamentary means to win the limited self-government known as Home Rule. In this 'New Departure' Fenians and MPs would work together to achieve greater tenant security in the short term, and peasant land-ownership and Irish self-government in the long term. In 1879 the Fenian agitator Michael Davitt founded the Land League, and the constitutionalist MP, Charles Stewart Parnell, became its first President. The leaders advocated peaceful means, but the followers were often more violent. Davitt, looking back on the 'Land War' of 1879 to 1882 in later years, justified the violence, but many in Britain thought such actions could never be justified.

Agrarian outrages appeared almost daily in the British newspaper columns.

4.12

> News of a terrible outrage reached Kanturk on Thursday ... a
> number of men disguised and armed entered the dwelling-house of a
> farmer ... put himself and his furniture on the roadside, beat him
> severely, and cut off his ears. The outrage is stated to be of an
> agrarian character, the man having, it is alleged, gone into possession 5
> of the house and lands adjoining immediately on the eviction of the
> party who had previously occupied them.

Morning Post, 9 October 1880

4.13

> A landlord named Hutchinson, residing near Skibbereen, was fired at
> from behind a fence as he was driving along the road on Saturday,
> and the driver ... was killed on the spot. Mr Hutchinson escaped. He
> was returning home from collecting rent ...
> ... It occurred in broad daylight, in the almost immediate vicinity of 5
> several houses, within a mile and a half of a police barrack, in the
> presence of at least one person, and within hearing distance of several
> others. The attacking party consisted of one man armed with a
> double-barrelled gun, the attacked of two men armed with revolvers,
> and yet the assassin escaped up a small rugged hill into a wood 10
> without a shot being fired ...

Morning Post, 18 and 19 October, 1880

4.14   Davitt defends the Land League methods of 1879 to 1880

It was the power of landlordism to demoralize which was its most
hateful feature. It owned the law, it influenced the churches, it
terrorized the homes of those on whose earnings it alone subsisted,
and in addition arrogated to its members a status of social superiority
which taught the landlord class to despise the very people by whom   5
and upon whom they lived. Against this enemy, therefore, it
was necessary to employ every force which we could influence or
employ ...
      Eviction has ever been the fruitful source of agrarian murder in
Ireland and, as the landlords were resolved to rely upon this kind of   10
warfare rather than upon Mr Gladstone's and Mr Forster's suggested
compromise, they were the direct instigators of the savage conflict
which was again to mark with traces of blood the tragic pathway
leading to Irish land reform.

Michael Davitt, *The Fall of Feudalism in Ireland*, 1904, pp. 188 and
269

4.15   Gladstone explains why stronger measures of coercion were needed in Ireland

In the second quarter of 1880 the meetings of the Land League, for
what reason I know not, fell to 31; and sure enough the agrarian
outrages went down with the meetings to 247. But in the third
quarter of 1880 the meetings of the Land League became very
frequent indeed; they rose to 137, and the agrarian outrages rose to   5
354. In the fourth quarter of 1880 the meetings of the Land League
were more than double – nearly treble. They rose from 137 to 392,
and the agrarian offences rose from 354 to 1,671, the evictions in the
meantime having enormously diminished, and having been in that
quarter only about one-fourth of what they had been before ...   10

Hansard, 28 January 1881, vol. 257, 1696

4.16   *The Times* condemns the Irish agitation

The very foundations of civilized life, as it is understood throughout
Western Europe, are being shaken in Ireland. Life is rendered in-
secure, its sustenance is withheld, the occupation of thousands is so

impeded that their very existence becomes precarious, property is
rendered valueless, contract is defied, and there remains hardly any   5
act of lawlessness for the followers of the Land League to commit,
unless it be the refusal to pay the QUEEN's taxes. No agrarian
distress, no hereditary grievance can justify such a complete defiance
of all the securities of civil and social life.

Anonymous editorial in *The Times*, 9 December 1880

Questions

1   To what practice does *The Times* refer when claiming 'sustenance is
withheld, the occupation of thousands is so impeded that their very
existence becomes precarious' [**4.16, lines 3–4**]?
2   What do **4.12** and **4.13** indicate about the nature of the agrarian
violence and the difficulties of governing Ireland?
3   What is Davitt's justification for the violent actions [**4.14**], and on
what grounds does *The Times* claim they are unjustifiable [**4.16**]?
4   Evaluate **4.14** and **4.15** as explanations for the violence. How far does
Gladstone undermine the basis of Davitt's arguments and in what
different ways can his statistics be interpreted?
5   How useful is *The Times* editorial [**4.16**] as a source on the nature of
agitation?
6   In September 1880 Parnell told an Irish meeting that 'the measure of
the land bill of next session will be the measure of your activity and
energy this winter'. In October the Liberal *Daily News* claimed that
the violent language of the Parnellites had 'estranged many a Liberal
Englishman from the cause which such speakers profess to represent'.
How far did violence gain concessions for the Irish tenantry?
7   In your opinion, can violence such as that reported in **4.12** and **4.13**
be justified, as Davitt suggests?

Home Rule

In October 1880 Gladstone wrote to the Chief Secretary for Ireland: 'Do
not suppose I dream of reviving the Irish Parliament; but ... I am
surprised at the narrowness of the case, upon which that Parliament was
condemned ...' Subsequent events, he thought, showed that English rule
was unacceptable to the Irish: the law was discredited as it came to the
people 'with a foreign aspect and in a foreign garb'. Agrarian outrages
still continued after the Second Land Act, and the arrest of Land League
leaders, including Parnell, failed to stop these. Although Parnell was later

released in 1882 on an understanding that he would use his influence to call off the violence, the murder of a new Chief Secretary for Ireland in Dublin's Phoenix Park, and the British government's continued use of coercion, depriving the Irish of many normal civil rights, exemplified the dangerous and unsatisfactory nature of English government in Ireland. This must have been further emphasised for Gladstone when Irish MPs brought down his government in 1885 and the ensuing Conservative administration decided that coercion should not be continued. After 1881 Gladstone had never spoken against Home Rule, and by late 1885 he came to believe it should be granted – but when and by whom? After his son Herbert revealed his views on the issue in December 1885 Gladstone formed a ministry to examine the practicality of Home Rule in early 1886. His First Home Rule Bill was introduced in the Spring amidst furious controversy.

4.17 Parnell argues that Home Rule will strengthen the Empire

We can point to the fact that under 85 years of parliamentary connexion with England, Ireland has become intensely disloyal and intensely disaffected ... We can show that disaffection has disappeared in all the greater English colonies, that while the Irishman who goes to the United States of America carries with him a burning hatred of   5
English rule ... the Irishman ... who goes to one of the colonies of Canada or one of the colonies of Australia, and finds there another and a different system of English rule to that which he has been accustomed to at home, becomes to a great extent a loyal citizen and a strength and a prop to the community amongst whom his lot has   10
been cast ...

Parnell speaking at Wicklow, 5 October 1885, from 'The Freeman's Journal', printed in E. Curtis and R. B. McDowell (ed.) *Irish Historical Documents*, 1943, pp. 285–86

4.18 Lord Salisbury condemns Home Rule at a Conservative banquet

We are asked to give up to two thirds, it may be, of Ireland one-third of its inhabitants, landowners, educated men, bankers, merchants, students, men of every class, who have loyally maintained the union, who have acted on the assumption that the Union was to be perpetual, who have avowed an English partisanship, have treated it as   5

their greatest honour and trusted in it as their greatest safety, and to
whom it will be, if you now abandon them, condemnation to utter
and certain ruin [Cheers] ...

There are other countries in the world where your Empire is
maintained by the faith which men have that those who take your   10
side will be supported and upheld. Whenever the thought crosses you
that you can safely abandon those who for centuries have taken your
side in Ireland, I beseech you to think of India ('Hear' and cheers). I
beseech you to think of the effect it will have if the suspicion can get
abroad there that, should convenience once dictate such a policy,   15
they, like the Loyalists of Ireland, will be flung aside like a sucked
orange when their purpose has been fulfilled [Cheers] ...

The Times, 18 February 1886

**4.19   Gladstone, defending his Bill, in an heroic three and a half
hour speech in the Commons**

Out of the six last centuries, for five centuries at least Ireland has had
a parliament separate from ours. That is a fact undeniable. Did that
separation of parliament destroy the unity of the British Empire? Did
it destroy it in the 18th century? ...

It was, in a pre-eminent sense, the century of Empire, and it was   5
in a sense, but too conspicuous, the century of wars. Those wars were
carried on, that Empire was maintained and enormously enlarged,
that trade was established, that Navy was brought to supremacy when
England and Ireland had separate parliaments. Am I to be told that
there was no unity of empire in that state of things?   10

Hansard, 8 April 1886, vol. 304, 1045

4.20

TEMPTATION OF THE GOOD ST. GLADSTONE.

Cartoon from *Punch*, 9 January 1886

Questions

1   On what grounds and how convincingly does Parnell argue that Home Rule will strengthen the Empire and Salisbury that Home Rule will weaken it [**4.17, 4.18**]?

2   Salisbury claimed that a third of the Irish people opposed Home Rule [**4.18**]
   (i) What does he indicate about the social composition of these 'Unionists'?
   (ii) How accurate are his indications?

3   How convincing is Gladstone's historical argument that Home Rule will not undermine the Empire [**4.19**]?

4   Identify as many figures as possible in the cartoon. [**4.20**]. What does the woman represent, and why is she covering her face with a mask?

5   A leading Conservative, Lord Randolph Churchill, condemned the Home Rule scheme as a base and nefarious 'conspiracy against the honour of Britain and the welfare of Ireland'. With reference to **4.18** and **4.20** explain why many critics regarded the Home Rule Bill as not only misguided but wicked.

6   Why did the maintenance of Empire seem so important in 1886? Support your answer from your wider reading.

5 The Eastern Question

The dilemma of the Eastern Question was what to do about the decaying Turkish Empire which extended across much of south-eastern Europe, the Middle East and North Africa. It was complicated by Russian and Austrian ambitions to expand in south-eastern Europe; the nationalism of Slav peoples in the area; and the moral and social problems of Moslem Turks ruling Christian Europeans. The British were concerned about trade routes and strategic positions in the eastern Mediterranean. British exports to Turkey had greatly increased in the mid 19th century, and the Suez Canal, opened in 1869, now formed a key link with India.

The London Conference, 1871

The traditional British response to the Eastern Question was to prop up Turkey and resist Russian expansion in the Turkish Empire. This policy had been put into effect in the Crimean War (1854–6) and upheld by Lord Palmerston. In an attempt to safeguard Turkish lands against Russian attack, the Treaty of Paris at the end of the Crimean War included an international agreement neutralising the Black Sea so that it should contain no sizeable warships or naval bases. But following the Franco–Prussian War of 1870, Russia declared that she would not be bound by the neutrality agreement. Gladstone's response was to call a conference in London where Britain accepted the Russian action.

Was the conference the right response? Was the Prime Minister's action strong enough? Gladstone and Disraeli clashed over the issue in a Commons debate in February 1871 during the conference. The *Punch* cartoonist comments on Gladstone's position in **5.1**. The artist refers back to a famous *Punch* cartoon of 1851, entitled the 'Judicious Bottle-holder' which showed Palmerston assisting those threatened by despotic rulers just as a man in the boxing ring revives fighters with a bottle of smelling salts. Turkey had been one of the states he helped in this way when it came under pressure from the Russian Tsar to give up political refugees and allow Russian interference within its Empire.

5.1

PUNCH, OR THE LONDON CHARIVARI.—February 25, 1871.

THE IN-"JUDICIOUS BOTTLE-HOLDER."

Ghost of Pam. "AHA, DEAR BOY! WE MANAGED THINGS RATHER DIFFERENTLY WHEN *I* WAS BOTTLE-HOLDER!"

"I have been told that Lord Palmerston always looked on the Neutralisation of the Black Sea as an arrangement that might be maintained for a limited number of years, but which it was impossible to maintain permanently. I have been told Lord Clarendon never attached value to that neutralisation."—Mr. Gladstone (while the Black Sea Conference was sitting).

Cartoon from *Punch*, 25 February 1871

5.2   Disraeli's View

I cannot understand, or conceive it possible, that a British Minister, after the immense sacrifices made by the Allies, and especially by this country, in order to obtain that Treaty of 1856, will consent in conference to give up the whole point for which those sacrifices were incurred. There really is nothing in the Treaty of 1856 of vital   5 importance ... except the termination of the naval preponderance of Russia in the Black Sea ... To obtain that result the Allies expended three hundred millions of treasure. I cannot trust myself to tell what was the loss in human lives, infinitely more valuable. You fought four pitched battles and made two of the most terrific assaults ever known   10 in the history of sieges, and all to obtain this result. Why, there is hardly a family in England, from the haughtiest to the humblest, which has not some painful recollection of the sufferings and sacrifices of that war ...

Hansard, 9 February 1871, vol. 204, 84

5.3   Gladstone's reply

In this House, in the year 1856, I declared my confident conviction that it was impossible to maintain the neutralization of the Black Sea ... I have been told that Lord Palmerston always looked upon the neutralization as an arrangement which might be maintained and held together for a limited number of years, but which, from its character,   5 it was impossible to maintain as a permanent condition for a great settlement of Europe ... Who is it that you would have looked to in order to maintain [Disraeli's] policy in the East, if matters now stood again as they were? France. But France by official acts expressed her readiness to give up the neutrality of the Black Sea. Which is the   10 Power most disposed to go with us in maintaining the spirit of the Treaty of 1856? The Austro-Hungarian Government. But they several years ago proposed to Russia that the Treaty should be altered, and that the neutrality of the Black Sea should be abandoned; and it is in this state of things that the right hon. Gentleman finds it   15 necessary ... to show how wrong we were not to go to war single-handed in order to force on Russia the permanent contraction of her rights of sovereignty over a portion of her territory ...

Hansard, 9 February 1871, vol. 204, 104–5

5.4   The Foreign Secretary, Lord Granville, listed the 'Alternatives to Conference' in a Memorandum of 30 March 1871. One of them was war:

2 Declaration of an offensive war deprecated by Turkey against a nation which like ourselves has peculiar advantages for defence – a war which could only have been undertaken by finding money and arms for Turkey, and for an object for which in all probability no country would have joined us excepting France, who has had another 5 object in view. (Nearly all the co-signatories of the Treaty of 1856 having said something in favour of revision [)].

Memorandum by Lord Granville, 30 March 1871, printed in
A. Ramm (ed.) *The Political Correspondence of Mr Gladstone and Lord Granville* 1868–76, vol. I, pp. 229–30

Questions

1   What does the cartoonist think of the way Gladstone's government handled the Russian action over the Black Sea [5.1]?
2   What is Disraeli's argument and what kind of response is he suggesting to Russia's action [5.2]?
3   How do Gladstone and Granville suggest his approach was unrealistic [5.3, 5.4]?
4   Who was more in line with Palmerston's thinking, Gladstone or Disraeli? Give reasons for your answer.
5   Which side of the argument would you have supported in 1871 and for what reasons?

The Bulgarian Atrocities

The Eastern Question again pressed on European governments' attention when Slav inhabitants of Bosnia and Herzegovina revolted against Turkish rule in 1875. When revolt spread to Bulgaria in 1876 and the Turks used irregular troops – Bashi-Bazouks – against the rebels, the resulting 'Bulgarian Atrocities' became an international scandal. These were first revealed in Britain in a report published on 23 June in the Liberal newspaper, the *Daily News*. The report came from its correspondent in Constantinople, Pears, who in turn relied on two former American missionaries, Washburn and Long, who taught at a college in the Turkish capital and gained information from their Bulgarian students.

5.5   Pears' report, published anonymously, in the *Daily News*

Dark rumours have been whispered about Constantinople during the
last month of horrible atrocities committed in Bulgaria... These cruelties have not been altogether (though they have in the main) confined
to the side of the Turks; but that which throws the balance altogether
against the latter is that the Government has been either unable or   5
unwilling to prevent its own employés – I am unwilling to use the
word soldiers, for the Bashi-Bazouks, by whom they have been
committed, are altogether unworthy of the name – from committing
these cruelties ... Composed of the dregs of the Turkish and Circas-
sian population, with gipsies and gaolbirds let out for the purpose,   10
and under no responsible command, they have been let loose upon a
large portion of central Bulgaria to put down the insurrection in their
own fashion. The result is what everybody acquainted with the
materials composing such a force might expect – the plundering of all
movable property, the burning of the houses and villages of the   15
peasantry, without the slightest regard to the question whether the
occupants have taken part in the insurrection or not, and the almost
indiscriminate slaughter of old men, women and children. One of the
most fertile and productive provinces of the Turkish Empire is thus
being laid waste ... It is too soon yet to attempt to ascertain, with any 20
degree of exactness, the number who have been killed. An intelligent
Turk who has just arrived estimates it at 18,000. Bulgarians speak of
30,000 and of the destruction of upwards of a hundred villages. I pass
over the stories of the burning of forty or fifty Bulgarian girls in a
stable and the massacre of upwards of a hundred children in the   25
village school-house, surprised by the Bashis, because though they are
repeated everywhere in Constantinople I have no sufficient authority
to enable me to express an opinion on their truth. The places where
these atrocities are said and generally believed to have occurred have
been utterly destroyed, and possibly also the evidence of the cruelties 30
which preceded their destruction. I have, however, trustworthy information of a number of other outrages, many of which are altogether
unfit for publication ...

   The difficulty of obtaining accurate statistics will be appreciated
when it is remembered that immediately upon the outbreak of the   35
troubles in Bulgaria the mails were placed under the strictest super-
vision ... The local journals were forbidden to publish any correspondence from those districts. Restrictions were placed upon travel ...

The Bashi-Bazouks of the Moslem village of Justina – that is to
say, all the lowest roughs of the place – armed by Government, with   40
full permission to kill, violate and rob, determined to destroy Perush-
titza [a Christian village in Bulgaria] unless its inhabitants would
consent to surrender all the arms and ten of the leading families as
hostages ... No charge of disloyalty, still less any charge of open
rebellion, had been brought against it. Its one offence was that it was   45
Christian, and in consequence, as compared with a Turkish village,
rich. For this reason alone the armed Moslem rabble were let loose
against it and its unoffending inhabitants. The village was surrounded
and the inhabitants fired upon ... A portion of the Christians even
now consented to give up their arms, on being assured that they   50
would not be injured ... The unarmed inhabitants were attacked.
Some of them fled; others took refuge in the two churches of the
village. On the 11th of May Raschid Pacha arrived with a body of
troops. He ordered the Christians to surrender their arms. They
naturally requested to be allowed to retain them until the Bashi-   55
Bazouks had withdrawn ... Raschid at once took the part of the
Turks, and ordered the villagers to give up their arms. He thereupon
made an attack upon the church, and old men, women and children
were indiscriminately slaughtered. Every house in the village was
burnt, and on the 14th of May not a house existed ... a number of   60
women were carried off as legitimate prizes by the Bashi-Bazouks ...

Daily News, 23 June 1876

Questions

1   What specific allegations are made in 5.5 against Turkish irregular
    troops and the Turkish government?
2   How reliable would you have judged the report to be if you were
    reading it in 1876? How does the knowledge we now have about
    Pears' sources of information affect your evaluation of the report as
    an historian?
3   Which aspects of the report were particularly likely to arouse a
    reaction among English readers? Which groups would you expect to
    be most affected by it and why?
4   The British government had an embassy in Constantinople and a
    vice-consul at Adrianople, south of Bulgaria: there was a telegraphic
    link with Constantinople and major towns in the Turkish Empire. (A

vice-consulate at Philippopolis in the area of the atrocities had
actually been removed by a Liberal government making economies in
British diplomatic representation in 1860.) What could the British
government have done to gain more information and what action do
you consider it should have taken over the report?

What the government actually did was send a copy of the *Daily News*
article to Sir Henry Elliot, the British ambassador in Constantinople, and
ask him to investigate the accusations. In fact Elliot had already received
early reports on the atrocities from the two Americans, Washburn and
Long, and from two British vice-consuls, but he did not send these on to
London, as they were unconfirmed and he doubted their accuracy. Elliot
normally took a favourable line towards the Turkish government. He
first sent a full report of what he knew about the 'atrocities' in a letter of 6
July, received in London on the 14th. The telegram in 5.7 followed. On
the same day Derby, the Foreign Secretary, instructed Elliot to 'urge' the
Turkish government 'strongly' to repress the outrages and ordered the
vice-consul at Adrianople to visit the area concerned to find out the
truth. Early reports from the vice-consul and another British diplomat,
Baring, were available when Disraeli spoke on 11 August.

5.6   From Disraeli's reply in the Commons to a question on the Atrocities, 10 July 1876

That there have been proceedings of an atrocious character in
Bulgaria I never for a moment doubted. Wars of insurrection are
always atrocious. These are wars not carried on by Regular troops –
in this case not even by Irregular troops – but by a sort of *posse
comitatus* of an armed population ... I cannot doubt that atrocities   5
have been committed in Bulgaria; but that girls were sold into
slavery, or that more than 10,000 persons have been imprisoned, I
doubt. In fact, I doubt whether there is prison accommodation for so
many, or that torture has been practised on a great scale among an
Oriental people who seldom, I believe, resort to torture, but generally 10
terminate their connection with culprits in a more expeditious manner. These are circumstances which lead me to hope that in time we
may be better informed ...

Hansard, 10 July 1876, vol. 230, 1181–82

5.7   Telegram from the British Ambassador to Turkey, Sir Henry Elliot, on 14 July 1876

We have no consular Agents except at Adrianople, Rustchuk and Bourgas, and they have seldom been able to guarantee the truth of the reports that reached them.

There can be no doubt that the instigators of the Insurrection began by committing atrocities on the Mussulmans and burning   5
Bulgarian villages with the view of creating exasperation between the two races. In this they succeeded and when BashiBazouks and Circas-
sians were called out they indulged in every kind of misconduct, killing and outraging many innocent persons.

I have been unable to verify the cases of wholesale slaughter that   10
have been brought forward which come mostly from quarters not entitled to much confidence.

A Bulgarian, at whose request I have several times made known to the Porte [Turkish Foreign Office] cases of maltreatment, assured me that the accounts published were grossly exaggerated, and he   15
expressly stated that he had no complaint to make of the conduct of the regular troops, but it appears from other sources that the regulars have at times been guilty of great excesses.

Bulgarian children certainly have been sold, but I cannot find that there has been anything like a regular traffic in them. Till I received   20
your telegram of yesterday I had heard nothing either of cartloads of heads being paraded, or of young women being publicly sold, but I will make every possible enquiry. It was supposed here that the abuses had been put a stop to for some time.

PRO FO78 2460 739

NEUTRALITY UNDER DIFFICULTIES.

Dizzy. "BULGARIAN ATROCITIES! I CAN'T FIND THEM IN THE 'OFFICIAL REPORTS'!!!!"

Cartoon from *Punch*, 5 August 1876

5.9   Disraeli replies to allegations about the atrocities and criticisms of the British government on 11 August 1876

There never were 40 maidens locked up in a stable and burnt alive. That was ascertained with great care by Mr Baring ... I believe, also, it is an entire fabrication that 1,000 young women were sold in the market as slaves... We know very well there has been considerable slaughter; that there must have been isolated and individual cases of   5 most atrocious rapine and outrages of a most atrocious kind; but still we have had communications with Sir Henry Elliot, and he has always assumed from what he knew that these cases of individual rapine and outrage were occurring ...

We are always treated as if we had some peculiar alliance with the   10 Turkish Government, as if we were their peculiar friends, and even as if we were expected to uphold them in any enormity they might commit. I want to know what evidence there is of that, what interest we have in such a thing. We are, it is true, the Allies of the Sultan of Turkey; so is Russia, so is Austria, so is France, and so are others ...   15

What our duty is at this critical moment is to maintain the Empire of England. Nor will we ever agree to any step, though it may obtain for a moment comparative quiet and a false prosperity, that hazards the existence of that Empire.

Hansard, 11 August 1876, vol. 231, 1141, 1145

Meanwhile, during August, an intense public agitation began against the atrocities manifesting, in Professor Shannon's words, 'the highest refinement of Victorian moral sensibility': on 28 August Gladstone felt 'called away' from the religious studies he had undertaken in semi-retirement 'to write on Bulgaria'. His pamphlet *The Bulgarian Horrors and the Question of the East* was published on 6 September.

5.10

We now know in detail that there have been perpetrated, under the immediate authority of a Government to which all the time we have been giving the strongest moral, and for part of the time even material support, crimes and outrages, so vast in scale as to exceed all modern example, and so unutterably vile as well as fierce in char-   5 acter, that it passes the power of heart to conceive, and of tongue and pen adequately to describe them. These are the Bulgarian horrors ...

W. E. Gladstone, *Bulgarian Horrors and the Question of the East*, 1876, pp. 11–12

1   What argument is the cartoon [5.8] advancing? How effective do you think it is in doing so?
2   What evidence does this section provide of inadequacy in the official reports? Using **5.6, 5.7** and **5.9**:
      (i) Was Disraeli's response justifiable in view of the information he received?
      (ii) How might the substance and phrasing of **5.6** and **5.9** be criticised on moral and humanitarian grounds?
      (iii) What was Disraeli's main concern in the crisis?
3   Bearing in mind the evidence in this chapter, do you think the British government was too slow in reacting to reports of the massacres?
4   From your further reading:
      How do Gladstone and Disraeli differ over the British government's responsibility for Turkish government actions? In what ways could the government be held to be giving the Turks 'moral' and 'material' support in 1876 [**5.10, lines 3–4**] and how far could the British government reasonably be held responsible for Turkish atrocities?

We shall never know how many Bulgarians died in the massacres. Baring, one of the British government's investigators, suggested 12,000, but he may well have over-estimated, not allowing for people who had fled their homes or migrated for summer work. Stoney, a railway engineer who subsequently made a house-to-house investigation, estimated 3,694.

The Congress of Berlin and beyond

Wider issues soon captured public attention. European attempts in 1876 to achieve Turkish administrative reforms and pacify the rebels all failed, and in April 1877 Russia went to war with Turkey to support their fellow Slavs and/or further Russian imperial ambitions. In early 1878 the Russians approached Constantinople: in March they virtually abolished the Turkish Empire in Europe by the imposed Treaty of San Stefano, and created a large Bulgaria which would then have a Russian army of occupation for a couple of years.

Public opinion became far more anti-Russian and pro-Turk, Disraeli made various military moves to threaten war and force the Russians to submit the whole of the San Stefano treaty to a European congress at Berlin. His new Foreign Secretary, Salisbury, then negotiated agreements with Russia, Austria and Turkey which reduced Russian land gains, restored some Turkish territory in Europe and brought Britain Cyprus in return for a new role in supporting Turkish power in Asia. These understandings formed the basis of a new settlement at the Congress of Berlin (June–July 1878): Disraeli had apparently achieved a great triumph, and Turkey, the 'Sick Man of Europe', though territorially slimmed down, had been given a new lease of life as a buffer against Russian penetration. But was this the right solution? Could the Turkish Empire be maintained and did it really serve British and European interests?

5.11   Gladstone's proposals for the Turkish Empire in 1876

The integrity of Turkey will be maintained by a titular sovereignty, verified as it were through a moderate payment of tribute, in order that Ottoman sovereignty may serve the purpose of shutting out from the present limits of the Turkish Empire any other sovereignty, or any exercise, in whole or in part, of sovereign rights by any other   5
Power, whether it be Russia on the Euxine, or Austria on the Danube, or France or England on the Nile and the Red Sea ...
  It is surely wise, then, to avail ourselves of that happy approach to unanimity which prevails among the powers, and to avert, or at the very least postpone, as long as we honourably can, the wholesale   10
scramble, which is too likely to follow upon any premature abandonment of the principle of territorial integrity for Turkey ... But even that crisis I for one would not agree to avert, or to postpone, at the cost of leaving room for the recurrence of the Bulgarian horrors ...

W. E. Gladstone, *Bulgarian Horrors and the Question of the East*, 1876, pp. 50 and 53

5.12   Salisbury in 1877

I feel convinced that the old policy – wise enough in its time – of defending English interests by sustaining the Ottoman dynasty has become impracticable, and I think the time has come for defending English interests in a more direct way by some territorial re-arrangement. I fear that when we come to do the same thing some years   5
later, one of two things will have happened. Either France will have

recovered her position and be jealous of any extension of our power
in the Mediterranean – or Germany will have become a naval power.
Either of these contingencies will make it difficult for us to provide
ourselves with a pied-à-terre in place of that which we shall infallibly   10
lose at Constantinople. Arrangements which may be easy now will be
impossible five years hence.

**Letter from Lord Salisbury to Lord Lytton, 9 March 1877, printed in
Lady Gwendolen Cecil, *Life of Robert, Marquis of Salisbury* vol. II,
1921, p. 130**

5.13   Disraeli in 1876

If the Russians had Constantinople, they could at any time march
their Army through Syria to the mouth of the Nile, and then what
would be the use of our holding Egypt? Not even the command of
the sea could help us under such circumstances. People who talk in
this manner must be utterly ignorant of geography. Our strength is   5
on the sea. Constantinople is the key of India, and not Egypt and the
Suez Canal.

**Memorandum by Lord Barrington recording Disraeli's views, 23
October 1876, printed in G. E. Buckle (ed.), *The Life of Benjamin
Disraeli, Earl of Beaconsfield*, vol. VI, 1920, p. 84**

5.14   Disraeli speaking in the House of Lords, 16 May 1879

Our objects were twofold. We wished to maintain Turkey as an
independent political State. It is very easy to talk of the Ottoman
power being at the point of extinction. But when you come practically to examine the question there is no living statesman who has
ever offered or propounded any practical solution of the difficulties   5
which would occur if the Ottoman Empire were to fall to pieces. One
result would probably be a long and general war, and that alone, I
think, is a sufficient reason for endeavouring to maintain as a State
the Ottoman Empire. But, while holding as a principle that the
Ottoman Empire must be maintained as a State, we have always been   10
of opinion that the only way to strengthen it was to improve the
condition of its subjects ...

**Printed in T. E. Kebbel (ed.), *Selected Speeches of the Earl of Beacons-
field*, vol. II, 1882, pp. 213–14**

5.15

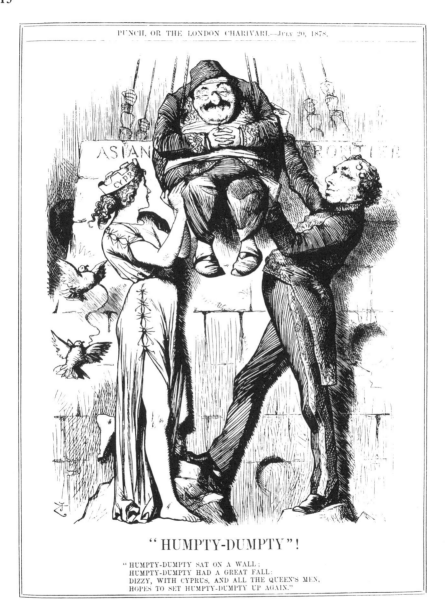

Cartoon from *Punch*, 20 July 1878

Questions

1   In what ways and for what reasons did Disraeli and his Foreign Secretary differ over the best policy to adopt towards Turkey [**5.12, 5.13, 5.14**]?

2   Compare the policies of Gladstone and Disraeli and their attitudes to Turkish government as expressed in **5.11** and **5.14**.

3   What argument is advanced in the cartoon [**5.15**] and with which statesman's view is it most compatible? Explain your answer.

4   **5.11** and **5.14** are public statements and **5.12** and **5.13** private ones. How does this affect their usefulness to the historian and how much of **5.12** and **5.13** could Salisbury and Disraeli have expressed publicly?

5   Which statesman's view appears most realistic, taking into account Turkey's history up to the end of World War 1? Justify your answer.

6 Empire

Attitudes to Empire

By the 1870s Britain already had an Empire on which 'the sun never set'. Although Europeans as yet controlled little of Africa, Britain had a vast Indian empire and large white settler colonies like Canada and Australia. Following the decisions of earlier governments, Gladstone's first ministry encouraged white colonists towards greater self-government, and withdrew imperial garrisons from Canada and New Zealand – a policy rousing much opposition among British imperial enthusiasts. While he was Chancellor of the Exchequer, Disraeli made some irritated remarks in private letters about colonies as expensive deadweights and 'a millstone round our necks' (letter from Disraeli to the Earl of Malmesbury, 1852). Publicly, however, he had long supported them as 'the surest sources' of our wealth and the 'most certain support' of our power. (Hansard, 15 June 1849). During 1872 he criticised the Liberal colonial policies of the previous 40 years in a major speech at the Crystal Palace: Gladstone subsequently attacked the developing imperialism of Disraeli's second ministry in a series of articles of the late 1870s.

6.1 Disraeli speaking on colonial administration at the Crystal Palace in 1872

Not that I for one object to self-government, I cannot conceive how our distant Colonies can have their affairs administered except by self-government. But self-government, in my opinion, when it was conceded, ought to have been conceded as part of a great policy of Imperial consolidation (Hear). It ought to have been accompanied by 5 an Imperial tariff, by securities for the people of England for the enjoyment of the unappropriated lands which belonged to the Sovereign as their trustee, and by a military code which should have precisely defined the means and the responsibilities by which the Colonies should have been defended, and by which, if necessary, this 10 country should call for aid from the Colonies themselves. (Hear, hear). It ought, further, to have been accompanied by the institution of some representative council in the metropolis, which would have

brought the Colonies into constant and continuous relations with the
Home Government. All this, however, was omitted, because those   15
who advised that policy – and I believe their convictions were
sincere – looked upon the Colonies of England, looked even upon our
connexion with India, as a burden upon this country, viewing everything in a financial aspect, and totally ignoring those moral and
political considerations which make nations great, and by the   20
influence of which alone men are distinguished from animals ... in my
opinion no Minister in this country will do his duty who neglects any
opportunity of reconstructing as much as possible our Colonial
Empire, and of responding to those distant sympathies which may
become the source of incalculable strength and happiness to this   25
land ...

The Times, 25 June 1872

6.2   From Gladstone's article on 'England's Mission' in 1878

Some seem actually to believe they are increasing strength, when they
multiply the points they are to occupy and defend, without adding a
single man to the force they can arm, or a pound to the fund by
which that force is to be sustained. But it is well to cherish no
illusions, and to look the matter in the face ...   5
Between the two parties in this controversy there is a perfect agreement that England has a mighty mission in the world; but there is a
discord as fundamental upon the question what that mission is.
    With one party, her first care is held to be the care of her own
children within her own shores, the redress of wrongs, the supply of   10
needs, the improvement of laws and institutions. Against this home-
spun doctrine, the present Government appears to set up territorial
aggrandisement, large establishments, and the accumulation of a
multitude of fictitious interests abroad, as if our real interests were
not enough ...   15
    The frame of mind is different, with which, from the two sides
respectively, our colonies are regarded. It is the administrative connection, and the shadow of political subordination, which chiefly gave
them value in the sight of the party, who at home as well as abroad
are striving to cajole or drive us into Imperialism. With their oppo- 20
nents, it is the welfare of these communities which forms the great
object of interest and desire; and if the day should ever come, when

in their view that welfare would be best promoted by their administrative emancipation, then and then only the Liberal mind of England would at once say, 'Let them flourish to the uttermost; and, if their 25 highest welfare requires their severance, we prefer their amicable independence to their constrained subordination.'

The Nineteenth Century, **September 1878**

Questions

1 What do you understand by an 'Imperial tariff' [**6.1, line 6**]?

2 Identify the main differences between Gladstone's and Disraeli's views on the importance of Empire and Britain's connections with her colonies [**6.1** and **6.2**].

3 How far does **6.1** suggest that Disraeli was concerned with 'territorial aggrandisement' and 'political subordination'?

4 To what extent does Gladstone view our colonies 'in a financial aspect' [**6.2**]?

5 To what extent was Disraeli proclaiming a policy for the future or a criticism of the past at the Crystal Palace?

6 Which source is most in line with general British thinking in (i) the later Victorian period and (ii) the late 20th century? Explain your answer.

Afghanistan

Liberal and Conservative ministries both faced problems on the borders of the Empire. A military expedition on the West African Gold Coast during Gladstone's first ministry led to an Ashanti War which Disraeli condemned in his 1874 election address as 'a costly and destructive contest'. However, his own difficulties in South Africa and Afghanistan late in his second ministry were far worse.

Afghanistan, on India's north-western frontier, was an important buffer state against the Russians. The new Indian Viceroy, Lord Lytton, tried to persuade the Afghan ruler (the Amir Sher Ali) to receive a British mission at his capital, Kabul, but without success. Lytton was therefore worried by reports of a Russian mission at Kabul in Summer 1878 and now wanted to insist on the Amir receiving a British one.

6.3   Telegram from Lord Cranbrook, the Secretary of State for India, to Lord Lytton, 3 August 1878

ASSUMING the certainty of Russian officers at Kabul, your proposals to insist on reception of British envoy approved ...

India Office MSS EUR E218/123 No. 46

Lytton made some very public preparations for dispatch of a mission to Kabul under General Sir Neville Chamberlain. On 19 August the Cabinet decided to send a diplomatic protest to Russia, but Cranbrook apparently did not inform Lytton until 13 September.

6.4   Telegram from India Office to Lytton, 13 September 1878

Official reply to remonstrance at St Petersburg on way to London. Important to receive this before Chamberlain starts ...

India Office L/PS/7/257, p. 168

Lytton still instructed Chamberlain to advance.

6.5   Telegram from Indian Government to Chamberlain, 19 September 1878

... Further delay is certainly most undesirable ... Early practical test of Amir's intentions desirable ...

India Office MSS EUR E218/123 No. 59 Enclosure 13

The mission was then turned back in the border regions of Afghanistan on the Amir's orders. As Salisbury, the Foreign Secretary, recognised Lytton had now 'got a snub which will make active measures inevitable.' In late October the Cabinet decided to send a full scale military expedition to invade Afghanistan.

6.6   From a letter from Cranbrook to Lytton, 6 October 1878

I had not disguised from you my surprise that you had started the mission before we knew the Russian reply and without telegraphing to me previously ... The Cabinet felt strongly on the subject as more

than one thought that the answer might have modified our course as
regarded Afghanistan ...   5

India Office MSS EUR E218/5

6.7   Disraeli's private view

I am not satisfied with the position, as nothing could justify Lytton's
course except he was prepared to act, and was in a situation which
justified the responsibility of disobeying the orders of HM
Government.

He was told to wait until we had received the answer from Russia   5
to our remonstrance. I was very strong on this, having good reasons
for my opinion. He disobeyed us ... He was told to send the Mission
by Candahar. He has sent it by the Khyber, and received a snub,
which it may cost us much to wipe away.

When V-Roys and Comms-in-chief disobey orders, they ought to   10
be sure of success in their mutiny. Lytton, by disobeying orders, has
only secured insult and failure ...

**Letter from Disraeli to Cranbrook, 26 September 1878, printed in
G. E. Buckle,** *The Life of Benjamin Disraeli, Earl of Beaconsfield*, **vol.
VI, 1920, p. 382**

6.8   Disraeli's public view

What was our difficulty with regard to Afghanistan? We could gain
no information as to what was going on beyond the mountain range
or what was preparing in the numerous valleys of Afghanistan. What
we wanted, therefore, was eyes to see and ears to hear, and we should
have attained our object had the Ameer made to us those concessions 5
which are commonly granted by all civilised States, and which even
some Oriental states do not deny us – namely, to have a minister at
his capital – a demand which we did not press – and men like our
consuls – general at some of his chief towns. That virtually would
have been a rectification of our frontier, because we should have got 10
rid of those obstacles that rendered it utterly impossible for us to
conduct public affairs with any knowledge of the circumstances with
which we had to deal as regarded Afghanistan ...

A scientific rectification of our frontier would effect for us all the
results we desired. And, my lords, what is a scientific frontier com-   15

pared with a haphazard one? Why, it is, as a great military authority has said, this – a scientific frontier can be defended with a garrison of 5,000 men, while with a haphazard one you may require an army of 100,000 men, and even then not be safe from sudden attack ...

Speech in the House of Lords, 10 December 1878, printed in T. E. Kebbel (ed.) *Selected Speeches of the Earl of Beaconsfield*, vol. II, 1882, p. 244

Gladstone condemned 'Beaconsfieldism' – what he saw as Disraeli's policy of extending and consolidating the Empire – in great campaigns in the Scottish constituency of Midlothian, first at a by-election in late 1879 and then in the 1880 General Election.

6.9   Gladstone refers to events in Afghanistan

Why was it that the Afghans were so jealous of the presence of a European Resident, which we think innocent enough? Because they were conversant with our practice in India, and because they knew that in India, wherever a European Resident was established, he was not a mere ambassador, but became the instrument through which   5
the independence of the State was destroyed, and the supremacy of Great Britain over it established. Whatever the Afghans may be, they are freemen like you; they value their freedom as you do; they gave their lives for their freedom as you would give your lives for yours ...
    What measures does this war entail upon your generals and   10
soldiers? It entails such measures as these, – that when in January 1879 they were making war among the mountain-tops of the passes between India and Afghanistan, the tribes who inhabited them, naturally and not wrongfully, issued forth from their villages to resist. And where they had so issued forth, the villages were burned to the   15
ground, and the women and the children, by natural and necessary consequence, driven forth to wander and to perish in the snow. These things, in my opinion, are horrible to the last degree ...

Gladstone's Sixteenth Midlothian speech at Penicuik, 25 March 1880, printed in W. E. Gladstone, *Political Speeches in Scotland*, vol. II, 1880, pp. 290 and 294

Questions

1   Why did the British government want to establish a mission in Afghanistan and why should the Afghan ruler resist this?

2   Why were British Cabinet ministers angry over Lytton's actions in sending the mission [**6.6** and **6.7**]?
3   Why would the government still support his actions publicly?
4   With reference to **6.2** and **6.9** examine the principles which underlay Gladstone's views on Imperialism.

Egypt and the Suez Canal

Britain was concerned with Egypt for two main reasons. Firstly, it contained the Suez Canal, the shorter, easier route for ships to India. Secondly, its government borrowed substantially from British investors. After the Egyptian ruler, Khedive Ismail, had stopped the repayment of large debts owed to creditors from many European countries in 1876, English and French commissioners attempted to reform Egyptian finances and control the government. On their insistence severe economies were made, and the Khedive was later replaced by his more compliant son Tewfik.

Gladstone warned against the dangers of occupying Egypt in an article, *Aggression on Egypt and Freedom in the East*, in 1877, predicting that an occupation would sour relations with France. But during his second ministry he was faced by an Egyptian nationalist revolt which developed in 1881 under the leadership of Arabi, an Egyptian army colonel. Arabi roused opposition against the Europeans and took effective control of the government. Amidst complex European and Oriental diplomacy the British and French sent a combined naval force towards the Egyptian port of Alexandria. The upshot was that the French withdrew, the British bombarded Alexandria, anti-European nationalist riots spread within Egypt and the British proceeded to conquer the country and take over the administration.

Why did Gladstone's government take a course he had previously condemned, and was it justified in doing so?

6.10   Gladstone speaking on the route to India at Glasgow, 1879

What is the meaning of safe-guarding the road to India? It seems to mean this; that a little island at the end of the world, having possessed itself of an enormous territory at the other end of the world, is entitled to say with respect to every land and every sea lying between its own shores and any part of that enormous possession, that it has a   5
preferential right to the possession or control of that intermediate

territory, in order, as it is called, to safe-guard the road to India. That, gentlemen, is a monstrous claim.

Speech at Glasgow, 5 December 1879, printed in W. E. Gladstone, *Political Speeches in Scotland,* **vol. I, 1880, p. 196.**

6.11   Gladstone explaining the government's aims in Egypt, 1882

The general maintenance of all established rights in Egypt, whether they be those of the Sultan, those of the Khedive, those of the people of Egypt, or those of the foreign bondholders, or whatever they may be – that, in fact, the single phrase, that we seek the maintenance of all established rights, and the provision of due guarantees for those   5
rights, is the description of the policy by which the Government is directed ...

Hansard, 14 June 1882, vol. 270, 1146–47

6.12   The Liberal Cabinet Minister, John Bright, resigned over the issue because of his doctrine:

That the moral law is intended not only for individual life, but for the life and practice of States in their dealings with one another. I think that in the present case there has been a manifest violation both of International Law and of the moral law, and therefore it is impossible for me to give my support to it ...   5

Hansard, 17 July 1882, vol. 272, 723

6.13   Another Liberal MP Sir Wilfred Lawson condemned government policy

He understood we were at war in order to restore the *status quo ante.* The *status quo ante* was the grinding down of the people of Egypt to obtain money for the bondholders of this country – nothing more nor less than an effort to pay the interest on the bondholders' money. The *status quo ante* was a control over the finances of the country,   5
which he maintained belonged to the people themselves; and for the Liberals, of all people, to engage in war to prevent people managing their own affairs was simply disgusting ...

It was liberty the Egyptian people wanted; they believed it was better to manage their own affairs ill than to have foreigners manag-   10 ing them well. That was what was generally called patriotism, and he could not understand why it was not to be regarded as a virtue in the case of these poor Egyptians ...

He always thought that the present Government had been put in power to alter the Tory policy, and now the argument was that they 15 must go on in the same way as the Tories began ...

Hansard, 25 July 1882, vol. 272, 1705–7

6.14   A prominent Conservative, Lord Randolph Churchill, attacks Gladstone

In Egypt, from the time when first a circle of financiers in London and Paris seduced Ismail Pasha into their net, and conveyed to him at different periods sums amounting to about eighty millions sterling, the whole strength of our Government appears to have been directed to fixing irrevocably upon the Egyptians the burden of these loans ... 5 It is sufficient to say, that of the eighty millions, the interest of which absorbs about two-thirds of the revenues of Egypt, the people of Egypt have not received, directly or indirectly, more than a·quarter; and if they had effected a successful revolution, and repudiated every single penny of these loans from beginning to end, so far from our 10 having the smallest right to interfere with them, we should rather be bound to approve their action ...

The other day the poor Egyptians were very near effecting a successful revolution; they were very near throwing off their suffocating bonds; but, unfortunately for us, Mr Gladstone... came upon 15 them with his armies and his fleets, destroyed their towns, devastated their country, slaughtered their thousands, and flung back these struggling wretches into the morass of oppression, back into the toils of their taskmasters. The revolution of Arabi was the movement of a nation ... 20

Speech at Edinburgh, 18 December 1883, printed in L. J. Jennings (ed.) *Speeches of the Rt Hon Lord Randolph Churchill MP*, vol. I, 1889, pp. 70–71

Questions

1   Gladstone was reluctant to order the bombardment of Alexandria but was outnumbered in the Cabinet. How did he justify the Egyptian campaign [**6.11**]?

2   Compare the values to which Gladstone, Bright and Lawson are appealing in **6.11, 6.12** and **6.13**.
3   Why did Lawson and Churchill claim the Egyptians were right to rebel [**6.13, 6.14**]?
4   How justified was Lawson's view that Gladstone's second ministry 'had been put in power to alter the Tory policy' and then argued 'that they must go on in the same way as the Tories began' [**6.13, lines 14–16**]?
5   Compare the tone and substance of Churchill's criticism [**6.14**] with Gladstone's condemnation of 'Beaconsfieldism' in Afghanistan [**6.9**]

General Gordon and the Sudan

Worse was to follow. The Khedive had ruled the Sudan and garrisoned it with some Egyptian troops, but this area was soon taken over by a Muslim religious revivalist known as the Mahdi. In early 1884 the British government sent Major General Charles Gordon, a keen Imperialist, zealous Christian and former Governor-General of the Sudan, to evacuate the garrisons. He went to the Sudanese capital of Khartoum, but was subsequently besieged by the Mahdi's forces: a relief expedition was sent but arrived too late. On 5 February 1885 came news that Khartoum had fallen: Gordon was dead. Were Gordon's instructions clear? Had he followed them? Did the government delay unjustifiably in sending a relief force and was Gladstone responsible for Gordon's death?

6.15   Gordon's instructions from the Foreign Secretary, Lord Granville

Her Majesty's Government are desirous that you should proceed at once to Egypt to report to them on the military situation in the Soudan, and on the measures which it may be advisable to take for the security of the Egyptian garrisons still holding positions in that country, and for the safety of the European population in Khartoum.   5
You are also desired to consider and report upon the best mode of effecting the evacuation of the interior of the Soudan, and upon the manner in which the safety and the good administration by the Egyptian Government of the ports on the sea coast can best be secured.   10

In connection with this subject you should pay especial consideration to the question of the steps that may usefully be taken to

counteract the stimulus which it is feared may possibly be given to
the Slave Trade by the present insurrectionary movement and by the
withdrawal of the Egyptian authority from the interior.   15
    You will be under the instructions of Her Majesty's Agent and
Consul Genl at Cairo ...
    You will consider yourself authorized and instructed to perform
such other duties as the Egyptian Government may desire to intrust
to you and as may be communicated to you by Sir E Baring ...   20

PRO FO 78 3696, Letter from the Foreign Office, 18 January 1884

6.16   Instruction from Sir Evelyn Baring

You will bear in mind that the main end to be pursued is the
Evacuation of the Soudan ...
I understand also that you entirely concur in the desirability of
adopting this policy, and that you think it should on no account be
changed ...   5

PRO FO 78 3666 No. 100, 25 January 1884

6.17   The Khedive's letter to Gordon

We do hereby appoint you Governor General of the Soudan by
reason of your perfect knowledge of that country, and we trust that
you will carry out our good intentions for the establishment of justice
and order, and that you will assure the peace and prosperity of the
peoples of Soudan by maintaining the security of the roads open to   5
Commerce ...

PRO FO 78 3666 No. 113, Translation of letter dated 26 January 1884

6.18   A British newspaper report, February 1884

CAIRO, FEB 23 (7:50 pm)

General Gordon has issued a manifesto from Khartoum, informing
the insurgents that the Sultan, 'the Commander of the Faithful',
intends to despatch a great army to conquer the country. He exhorts
them to accept his offers of peace in order to preserve themselves
from Turkish invasion.   5

The Observer, 24 February 1884

Khartoum was besieged from March 1884.

6.19   Part of a dispatch from Baring to Granville, 26 March 1884

Let me earnestly beg Her Majesty's Government to place themselves
in the position of General Gordon and Colonel Stewart. These
officers have been sent on a most difficult and dangerous mission by
Her Majesty's Government. Their proposal that Zobeir Pasha should
be sent to Khartoum, which, if it had been acted on some weeks ago,   5
would, without doubt, have entirely altered the situation, was
rejected: and the consequences which they foresaw have ensued ...

PRO FO 78 3669 No. 362

6.20   From the draft of a dispatch from Granville to Baring, 28 March 1884

The circumstances with which it was necessary to deal were, no
doubt, difficult, and might change from day to day, but it certainly
was not in contemplation that the duties to be assigned to General
Gordon should be of a nature which would require the dispatch of a
British expedition to support or to extricate him ...   5

PRO FO 78 3662 No. 192B

Preparations for a relief force were made during August, but Gladstone
delayed its departure and on 16 September Wolseley, the officer in
charge, was warned not to move unless it was absolutely necessary. He
was finally ordered to advance on 25 September.

6.21   From Gordon's journal, 24 September 1884

I altogether *decline* the imputation that the projected expedition has
come to *relieve me*. It has *come to* SAVE OUR NATIONAL
HONOUR *in extricating the garrisons, etc, from a position our action in
Egypt has placed these garrisons. I was relief expedition No 1.* They are
relief expedition No 2. As for myself I could make good my retreat at   5
any moment if I wished ... *I came up to extricate the garrisons and
failed. Earle comes up to extricate garrisons and (I hope) succeeds. Earle
does not come to extricate me.* The extrication of the garrisons was
supposed to affect our 'national honour.' If Earle succeeds the

'national honour' thanks him and I hope rewards him, but it is   10
altogether independent of me, who for failing incurs its blame. I am
not the *rescued lamb*, and I will not be.

The Journals of Major–Gen. C. G. Gordon at Kartoum, 1885, p. 93

6.22   The *Morning Post* reports the fall of Khartoum

Khartoum has fallen, and GORDON is either a prisoner or slain. Such
was the terrible message from the Soudan which fell yesterday like an
avalanche upon the country, and spread consternation in every British
home. At the very moment when a personal heroism unsurpassed in
the annals of history was confidently believed to have been crowned   5
with its fitting reward, at the very instant when unexampled courage,
intelligence, and endurance were about to be sealed by the vulgar
stamp of success, the crown was torn from the victor's brows by the
treachery of those for whom he had unselfishly sacrificed himself ...

Morning Post, 6 February 1885

Questions

1   With reference to **6.15, 6.16** and **6.17** examine how far Gordon's
instructions were ambiguous or contradictory.
2   Evaluate **6.18** as a piece of historical evidence. What does it suggest
about the way Gordon followed his instructions?
3   With reference to all the evidence in this section how far do you
agree with the *Morning Post*'s view [**6.22**] that Gordon had been
killed through the treachery of the government?
4   With reference to your wider reading, to what extent did the circumstances of Gordon's death harm Gladstone's political reputation?

Index